C A P S T O N E

MW00744080

Stay Smart!

Smart things to know about... is a complete library of the world's smartest business ideas. **Smart** books put you on the inside track to the knowledge and skills that make the most successful people tick.

Each book brings you right up to speed on a crucial business issue. The subjects that business people tell us they most want to master are:

*Smart Things to Know about **Brands & Branding**,* JOHN MARIOTTI

*Smart Things to Know about **Business Finance**,* KEN LANGDON

*Smart Things to Know about **Change**,* DAVID FIRTH

*Smart Things to Know about **Customers**,* ROS JAY

*Smart Things to Know about **Decision Making**,* KEN LANGDON

*Smart Things to Know about **E-Commerce**,* MIKE CUNNINGHAM

*Smart Things to Know about **Innovation & Creativity**,* DENNIS SHERWOOD

*Smart Things to Know about **Knowledge Management**,*
TOM M. KOULOPOULOS & CARL FRAPPAOLO

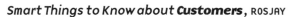

*Smart Things to Know about **Managing Projects**,* DONNA DEEPROSE

*Smart Things to Know about **Marketing**,* JOHN MARIOTTI

*Smart Things to Know about **Partnerships**,* JOHN MARIOTTI

*Smart Things to Know about **People Management**,* DAVID FIRTH

*Smart Things to Know about **Strategy**,* RICHARD KOCH

*Smart Things to Know about **Teams**,* ANNEMARIE CARACCIOLO

*Smart Things to Know about **Your Career**,* JOHN MIDDLETON

You can stay **Smart** by e-mailing us at **info@wiley-capstone.co.uk**
Let us keep you up to date with new Smart books, Smart updates, a Smart newsletter
and Smart seminars and conferences. Get in touch to discuss your needs.

CAPSTONE

Smart
THINGS TO KNOW ABOUT

Partnerships

JOHN MARIOTTI

Copyright © John Mariotti 2001

The right of John Mariotti to be identified as the author of this work has been asserted in accordance with the Copyright, Designs and Patents Act 1988

First published 2001 by
Capstone Publishing Limited (A Wiley Company)
8 Newtec Place
Magdalen Road
Oxford OX4 1RE
United Kingdom
http://www.capstoneideas.com

All rights reserved. Except for the quotation of short passages for the purposes of criticism and review, no part of this publication may be reproduced, stored in a retrieval system, or transmitted, in any form or by any means, electronic, mechanical, photocopying, recording or otherwise, without the prior permission of the publisher

CIP catalogue records for this book are available from the British Library and the US Library of Congress

ISBN 1-84112-112-6

Typeset in 11/15pt Sabon by
Sparks Computer Solutions Ltd, Oxford, UK
http://www.sparks.co.uk
Printed and bound by
T.J. International Ltd, Padstow, Cornwall

This book is printed on acid-free paper

Substantial discounts on bulk quantities of Capstone books are available to corporations, professional associations and other organizations. Please contact John Wiley & Sons for more details on 212 850 6000 or (fax) 212 850 6088 or (e-mail) info@wiley-capstone.co.uk

This book is dedicated to two people who have taught me more about partnerships than anyone else: my wife of 37 years, Maureen, and Jack Kahl, who personifies partnerships.

Contents

What is Smart?

The *Smart* series is a new way of learning. *Smart* books will improve your understanding and performance in some of the critical areas you face today like *customers, strategy, change, e-commerce, brands, influencing skills, knowledge management, finance, teamworking, partnerships.*

Smart books summarize accumulated wisdom as well as providing original cutting-edge ideas and tools that will take you out of theory and into action.

The widely respected business guru Chris Argyris points out that even the most intelligent individuals can become ineffective in organizations. Why? Because we are so busy working that we fail to learn about ourselves. We stop reflecting on the changes around us. We get sucked into the patterns of behavior that have produced success for us in the past, not realizing that it may no longer be appropriate for us in the fast-approaching future.

There are three ways the *Smart* series helps prevent this happening to you:

- by increasing your self-awareness;

- by developing your understanding, attitude and behavior; and

- by giving you the tools to challenge the status quo that exists in your organization.

Smart people need smart organizations. You could spend a third of your career hopping around in search of the Holy Grail, or you could begin to create your own smart organization around you today.

Finally a reminder that books don't change the world, people do. And although the *Smart* series offers you the brightest wisdom from the best practitioners and thinkers, these books throw the responsibility on you to *apply* what you're learning in your work.

Because the truly smart person knows that reading a book is the start of the process and not the end ...

As Eric Hoffer says, "In times of change, learners inherit the world, while the learned remain beautifully equipped to deal with a world that no longer exists."

David Firth
Smartmaster

Smart People to Have on Your Side

Jordan Lewis, PhD – former professor at the Wharton School of Business, and a leading consultant, lecturer and author of *Partnerships for Profit*, *The Connected Corporation*, and *Trusted Partners*, all published by The Free Press.

Yves Doz and Gary Hamel – authors of *Alliance Advantage*, Harvard Business School Press, 1998. Hamel is also the author of the best-seller *Leading the Revolution* and co-author with C. K. Prahalad of *Competing for the Future*. He is founder of Strategos, a strategic consulting company, and a professor at the Harvard Business School and the London Business School. Doz is a professor at INSEAD, and has held faculty positions at Harvard and Stanford.

Ray Mundy, PhD – Barriger Distinguished Professor of Transportation and director of the Center for Transportation Studies at the University of Missouri, St Louis (rmundy@umsl.edu). He is also executive director of the

Airport Ground Transportation Association, director of the Tennessee Transportation and Logistics Foundation, and a consultant to leading corporations such as John Deere, TNT Logistics and many others.

Stephen Dent – founding partner of The Partnership Continuum consulting organization (www.partneringintelligence.com), and an award-winning organizational consultant. Author of *Partnering Intelligence – Creating Value for Your Business by Building Strong Alliances* (Davies-Black 1999).

Robert Rogers – president and COO, Development Dimensions International, an author, speaker and consultant to leading global companies such as Caterpillar Tractor, Georgia-Pacific, Ford Motor, Kemper Insurance and many others (www.ddiworld.com).

Peter F. Drucker – author, consultant and perhaps the greatest management thinker of the 20th century. Author of numerous books including *The Concept of the Corporation, The Practice of Management, Managing in Turbulent Times, Management Challenges for the 21st Century* and many others.

The Six Smartest Things to Know about Partnerships

No one is good enough to succeed alone. You can run but you can't hide from problems – seek help.

Whoever chooses the best partners, wins! Choosing your partners carefully is the most important decision of all.

Trust is a must – and a two-way street. Never, ever doublecross your partner!

There has to be enough in it for both partners. Risks and rewards must be balanced too. Lopsided partnerships topple from their own imbalance.

No support from the top means no deal. Ultimately, lack of top to bottom commitment is usually an insurmountable obstacle to success in partnerships.

Power is poison to partnerships. The use of power, creating win-lose situations is a sure path to failure. Don't do it – even if/when you have the "power."

Preface

Think back to your childhood. Most of you can recall a close friend or relative who was your special "partner." You did things together, confided in each other and trusted each other implicitly. There was passion in your attempts to do the new or seemingly impossible, and share the exhilaration of success. Remember the feeling of closeness and the satisfaction of having someone to tackle problems with, enjoy adventures with, celebrate or grieve with, and generally share your life's journey. If you can recall clearly, you probably also remember that the values you shared were similar.

Values are deep-seated beliefs, principles, and behaviors that are developed over the years, as we grow and mature. These values are our guiding light, our rudder and a compass by which to steer our lives and actions – and our partnerships. Strong values create strong leaders, strong followers, and strong partners. When combined in a group of close-knit partners, the values-based culture that results is a very cohesive one. It is also one that can achieve its goals very effectively, and does so by forming powerful relationships – called partnerships – with other groups that complement its talents, skills, resources and capabilities.

I'd like to share a very personal partnership story that I told first in my earlier book, *The Power of Partnerships*. Nothing tells about partnerships quite so eloquently as real life.

In April 1983, I had the terrible task of telling my associates at the Huffy Oklahoma Bicycle Division, that our plant/division in Ponca City, OK was closing – through no fault of theirs. The company simply had too much bike capacity for the depressed market and the Ohio plant was the biggest and most mature, so it would be the survivor of the company's three plants/ divisions. I had seen the day coming for several months and dreaded it – I knew because I had agreed to go back to Ohio as president of the sole surviving division – Huffy Bicycles.

The morning consisted of four meetings. One with my direct staff, who pretty much knew what was happening; one with the remainder of the salaried work force; one with the "city fathers," who had been so supportive and cooperative over Huffy's three-plus years there; and finally one with the 500 hourly employees. These 500 were the "survivors" of a vigorous weeding out process; and they were good, loyal, hard working and productive people. Unfortunately, nothing they could have done would have kept the plant open.

The first meeting was not so bad, because my staff had been prepared. I got a little emotional, but kept it mostly under control. This second was a lot harder. The salaried group and I had been through a lot together. I broke down in tears, briefly. Then, after a couple of deep breaths, I answered questions for 30 minutes. The city leaders were next. These included some personal friends and people who had "gone the distance" to get us training help, tax abatement, a new road, and so on. It was a rerun of the salaried group meeting: some tears, some desperate pleas to see if they could help in any way to keep the plant open. The city would be losing its second largest employer. Finally, it was over.

Then came the really tough one – with the hourly workers. By this time, I knew the "grapevine" must have leaked word of the news to the plant, which was connected to the offices. I was surprised when I received a polite round of applause as I stepped to the podium. In spite of a lot of deep breaths and much resolve, I could not contain my emotions. I still get choked up writing about it.

These people had come from far and near, from farms and villages, a few even from the oil fields. They had survived all the startup troubles, from machine malfunctions to broken plumbing. They had struggled to learn how to build bicycles with a speed and precision that would measure up in a company widely regarded (at that time) as the most productive bike producer in the world. And they had done it! Quality was even better than in the mature Ohio plant, and productivity was close to that plant's levels.

SMART VOICES

"Simply put, you can't go it alone."

James Daly, editor-in-chief, Business 2.0

Now, because of some macro-economic reasons that I was going to try to explain, they would all be out of jobs soon. As I stood at the mike with tears streaming down my face, they waited patiently for me to tell them what they already knew was going to happen to them and why. Finally, I was able to get the words out. When I finished and prepared to leave the podium, I received another round of applause – this time not just polite but hearty applause. I was floored.

Over the three months that followed, I found that my partners in the factory had truly responded to my appeal to "go out in style." Quality improved. Productivity stayed high. Part of it was, no doubt, due to our superb vice-president of operations, John Simonis (now deceased) and the other management who had designed the plant, operated it through startup woes, had it humming, and then had to shut it down.

What does this personal story have to do with partnerships? It embodies the very essence of partnerships. We pulled together as partners. We were successful as partners. Employees, suppliers, customers, community – all were superb partners. And, when the time came to shut it down, we all shared the pain, the grief, and the pride as partners.

I left Ponca City, Oklahoma, about 18 years ago. That fateful day was April 13, 1983 – the day after my 42nd birthday. As I reflect back, I consider it to be an awful birthday that year, except for one thing – the support of and the partnership with the people of that plant. Their applause remains one of the saddest and strangely, of the happiest memories of my business career. In good times and bad, partners are still partners, and that is what they were telling me.

Smart quotes

"Without partnerships, how can we possibly compete tomorrow?"

Stephen M. Dent, *Partnering Intelligence*, Davies-Black 1999

There are other ways to achieve business goals; often it is done through control, power, fear, intimidation, manipulation, or outright deceit and dishonesty – "faking it." For several decades, this unprincipled, dishonest, valueless approach has yielded notable, temporary successes. It also made the word partnership into a bad joke or an overused cliché. That era is over now.

The recent era of the dot-com explosion and collapse exposed hundreds of flimsy partnerships and alliances. Most were as poorly thought out as the business ventures that spawned them. Those who have followed this ill-conceived path are now being punished at an increasing rate because of the pressure of rapid change and global

> "Trust is at the heart of today's knowledge economy."
>
> Jordan Lewis, *Trusted Partners*, The Free Press, 1999

SMART PEOPLE
TO HAVE ON
YOUR SIDE

competition. The phonies have been exposed, and the alliances they formed, which were not true partnerships – simply marriages of convenience – could not last. The apparent synergy they were striving for has dissipated in confusion, mistrust and defensive behavior.

But just because partnerships were misused and abused does not mean that they are worthless – far from it! The concept of partnership made great sense in the early stages of a fast-changing, cyberspace economy. It still does – maybe more so than ever. In *Smart Things to Know about Partnerships* you will learn why and how to make partnerships work for you and how to avoid most of the traps that caught many of your predecessors.

To form true partnerships, trust is the first and most essential ingredient. To make those partnerships really work, passion is the next and most magical

> "For as long as humans have populated this planet, we have struggled to survive. Along the way we learned that prosperity lay in banding together, determining what was in our best mutual interest, and moving forward in partnership. This strategy worked for thousands of years until the industrial age, when something fundamental changed in our society.
>
> "As the industrial workplace became fragmented, functionalized, and specialized, we began to transition from banding together to looking out for ourselves individually. We forgot the importance of relationships that valued the 'we' over the 'me' as our work drove us farther and farther apart."
>
> Stephen M. Dent, *Partnering Intelligence*, Davies-Black 1999

SMART PEOPLE
TO HAVE ON
YOUR SIDE

ingredient. I have been accused of being an expert on partnerships. I am not sure I want to claim that position. What I do want to claim is that I am personally passionate about partnerships because I have seen their power. Now let's start the journey together to discover many more smart things to know about partnerships.

1

Strategy in the New Economy

"NO TIME TO WAIT, NO PLACE TO HIDE"

THE SIX SMARTEST THINGS TO KNOW ABOUT PARTNERSHIPS

No one is good enough to succeed alone.
Whoever chooses the best partners, wins!
Trust is a must – and a two-way street.
There has to be enough in it for both partners.
No support from the top means "no deal."
Power is poison to partnerships.

A sea change underway

We are in the midst of a sea change in strategy and execution in the world of business. An explosion of computing and communications technology led by the Internet, but fed by the growth of globalization, is driving this *tsunami* of change. The faster we can compute and communicate, over greater distances and between more different cultures, the faster people must

Smart quotes

"Partnerships of all forms have become a central part of this new age."

James Daly

be able to gather information, respond to situations and make decisions.

Unfortunately, people are still people and are unprepared for this demand for fast, yet effective decisions and actions. Since it is unlikely that even genetic engineering will dramatically change the basic mental capabilities of the human race, how are people supposed to respond to these demands? One choice is to make fast decisions by "shooting from the hip" so to speak. Another is to not make decisions, but even indecision is a form of a decision.

How to take the actions that go with the decisions is equally perplexing. Everyone I talk to is time-starved and/or time-stressed. Information overload has become so pervasive that many people have simply given up. They use the same few resources over and over, with desperate disregard for the fact that there may be better ones available. Who has time to look for them? Maybe your competitors do!

Smart quotes

"The insatiable drive for efficiency and innovation as well as the ongoing acceleration of deregulation, global trade, and technological advancement has made partnering a necessary competitive strategy."

James Daly

There is simply no time to wait and no place to hide from this problem. Fortunately, there is an answer to this dilemma. Seek help! Radical idea, right? Somehow we think that asking for help or seeking help is a form of weakness! It isn't. It is a form of good sense and wise behavior. Help can come in many forms, but the most powerful, effective and humane form is that of partnerships, alliances and affiliations.

But partnership is such a cliché – or is it? Maybe "partnership" is an overworked word, but here I am writing about it … and here you are reading about it. Why? The best answer is in the old saw "misery loves company." When in desperate need, help is welcome indeed. But when conditions are "normal" (whatever that means these days), help is still valuable – for many reasons.

"The wonderful thing about partnership is that it halves your sorrow and compounds your joy."

Pat Summitt, basketball coach of the University of Tennessee Lady Vols 6-time National Championship Teams

SMART VOICES

Why partnerships are strategically necessary

In this chapter, I will try to give you some insights into how strategic partnerships are necessary, what they are, how complex the world has become for partnerships, and the role of people and information in forming strong partnerships. The strategy of partnerships has changed as complexity grows and technology spreads into what is now called the "New Economy." Age-old principles do not disappear or become useless; they simply have to be adapted to a new environment, which moves further and faster than ever before.

"… time to market and speed of integration are what's critical."

An investment banker, in "Merging at INTERNET SPEED," *Fortune*

"Only time will tell whether today's Net-speed haste makes even more waste. Or less."

Bethany McLean in "Merging at INTERNET SPEED," *Fortune*, November 8, 1999

Smart quotes

Fortunately, people are still the constant factor. Success in partnerships and alliances depends first on people and then on other factors. But the best of people will not succeed if ineffective strategies or non-competitive technologies hinder them. In succeeding chapters I will expand on these and other topics to help you learn more smart things to know about partnerships.

Smart quotes

"Fads will come and go. The fundamental fact of man's capacity to collaborate with his fellows in face-to-face groups will survive fads and one day be recognized. Then, and only then will management discover how seriously it has underestimated the true potential of its human resources."

Douglas McGregor in *The Human Side of Enterprise*

The name isn't the important thing

First of all, forget arguments about the name. I really don't care whether you call them partnerships, alliances, or a million other names. It doesn't matter so much what name you use, as how well you understand what it is you are talking about. Alliances are different from traditional partnerships, but both are interdependent and collaborative relationships in which two or more organizations agree to work together for some reasons that make sense to each of them. The larger difference between the names and the forms of these relationships has to do with the purposes, the commitment, the intended outcome and the motives of the participants.

SMART VOICES

"No company can go it alone ... if the 'capacity to collaborate' is not already a core competence in your organization, you had better get busy making it so."

Yves Doz and Gary Hamel

These partnerships and alliances come in all kinds, all sizes, shapes, motives, legal configurations, and so forth. But, when you boil them down to their essence, they are all about people working together to achieve something that is important to them – or not! Many of the quotes I have included refer to "alliances." Pay close attention to the differences that experts like Doz and Hamel use to differentiate alliances from partnerships. Contrast that with the "trust" so often referred to by Jordan Lewis in his discussions of partnerships.

Maybe a good way to differentiate a "true partnership" from a "convenient alliance" is by the measure of trust and commitment that it includes and depends on. Convenient alliances are more like affairs or liaisons (or one-night stands), whereas true partnerships are more like marriages.

KILLER QUESTIONS

How can we find the best possible partners to help us?

We all need partners!

The fact is that we all seek some kinds of relationships that fill out our life. God made Eve so Adam could have a partner. People marry because they want the love and companionship of a life partner. Companies have more practical reasons. Mostly, companies partner because they cannot do everything themselves.

Henry Ford tried it and for a while it worked. Ford owned the iron mines, the steel mills, the fabrication plants, the assembly plants and even the distribution system – for a while! Such "vertical integration" is unheard of in today's fast-moving, constantly changing global economy.

"These days, the third-party relationship is more like a marriage ..."

– Arnold Maltz, assistant professor, New Mexico State University in "Switch Partners or Keep Dancing?" *Transportation and Distribution*, July 1997

SMART VOICES

Smart things
to say

Nobody can be good enough at
everything – so what should we
get partners to be good at
for us?

Face it – partnerships, or whatever you call them, are necessary – no, they are critical to the success of companies everywhere. Some partners abuse each other. Some partnerships are shams. Others are short-lived. But some partnerships are real, meaningful, powerful and long-lasting. Even these have their periods of struggle and strife.

Most partnerships that fail were doomed almost from the start, because they started the wrong way. The hardest thing to do is to get a good partnership started in the right way. The next hardest thing to do is to keep a partnership going while maintaining a positive outlook and a collaborative spirit.

Partnership – many definitions

Before we go any further, let me define what I mean by a "partnership."

A partnership is an interdependent relationship between people and/or organizations in which they work together to achieve some mutual goals, and in which each invests resources and takes risks.

Many other people have defined partnerships in different ways, and I will tell you more about those as we move through the book. Because there are so many different kinds of relationships that are called partnerships, it is not

SMART VOICES

"… all too often, the underlying assumptions about the strategic logic of the alliance have been poorly tested and are more fantasy than reality."

Yves Doz and Gary Hamel

> "I use the term alliance to mean cooperation between groups that produces better results than can be gained from a transaction."
>
> Jordan Lewis

SMART PEOPLE
TO HAVE ON
YOUR SIDE

surprising for there to be many definitions. This is sort of like the blind men describing an elephant – it depends on which part you are talking about.

Another kind of partnership is the legal entity called a partnership. There will be a brief section devoted to this too, but smart readers know that *legal advice should come from lawyers* – so I will only give you the practical highlights of a partnership as a legal entity.

> "A partnership is an association with another entity in a joint endeavor, where both parties have joint interests, joint risks, and rewards."
>
> Clifford T. Lynch, "Managing the Outsourcing Relationship," *Supply Chain Management Review*, Sept–Oct, 2000

SMART VOICES

Partnerships and the Value Network

No one can be good enough at everything to succeed in today's dynamic global markets. The world in which we live and work is a very big, complex place. We actually have to work with this huge network – I call it a "Value Network." The Value Network encompasses the whole world and is a hugely complicated set of interconnected "things." But don't let that bother you, because like most large, complex things, we will break it down into smaller, more manageable parts before we try to do anything with it. After all, you wouldn't eat an elephant all in one bite would you? (Who'd eat an elephant at all? I wonder where these metaphors come from?)

KILLER QUESTIONS

Will the partnership
or the alliance create
value and for whom?

Let's start breaking down this Value Network into its pieces and see where partnerships fit. First, there is the old traditional "supply chain" or "value chain" – from the suppliers' suppliers through the customers' customers. It's really not a "chain" at all. It is a non-linear, complex network in itself. Try diagramming it and you'll see how complex it is.

The decisions are all made at the nodes of the network where the people are, even though most of the actual value is added in the links between the nodes, where material is flowing and work is done. Do you think partnerships are important in getting people who are spread across the nodes of a "supply chain network" to work together, to maximize the effectiveness of the entire network? Of course they are! That is the most important and challenging aspect of this time-honored tool, and the one that limits the performance of "supply chains" all over the world.

Thomas Friedman's fine book *The Lexus and the Olive Tree* describes the essence of globalization wonderfully. This term – globalization – is an apt name for the global, socio-political and economic situations that influence how and where value creation occurs on a massive scale. (Translation: what gets made where, and why.)

SMART VOICES

"Conventional partnerships serve set objectives and face well-circumscribed risks; their economics are usually clearly understood from the start, and their strategic scope is usually limited and clearly bounded ... Not so in the strategic alliance, in which the partners must be flexible and must see theirs as a relationship whose objectives are bound to evolve in ways that cannot be fully planned at the inception."

Yves Doz and Gary Hamel

"One reason the trend toward partnerships is accelerating is that no one company, not even the telephone giants, has enough money to swing the deal alone. A more important reason is that no one company has the needed technology."

Peter Drucker, "The Network Society," *Wall Street Journal*, March 29, 1995

SMART PEOPLE
TO HAVE ON
YOUR SIDE

Competition is global and anyone who ignores that fact won't be around long enough to finish reading this book! Whether you make something in Chicago, Chile or China makes a lot of difference. The partnership considerations in just those three choices are staggering. Imagine partnerships that span the globe, encompassing dozens of countries and cultures, with different regulations, tariffs, politics, social practices, cultures, religions, beliefs, … and economies – Whew! No wonder it is important to be "smart" about this global Value Network.

Next there is the information, communication and computing infrastructure, extending around the globe. Its span reaches from the fiber optic cables under the oceans to orbiting satellites in the stratosphere. This physical network is growing by leaps and bounds, and creating ever more potential for communications and computing growth. Moore's Law (the doubling, every 18 months, of performance per unit cost of microprocessor power) and Metcalfe's law (the exponentially increasing power of networks as the number of connected participants grows) are just our feeble attempts to quantify something that boggles our minds. But, the ideas these laws describe influence many of your business decisions – whether you like it or not, understand it or not.

KILLER QUESTIONS

Do we understand all of the aspects of this partnership network we are a part of?
Don't we have to?

SMART PEOPLE
TO HAVE ON
YOUR SIDE

"I used to teach about market-entry barriers at Wharton, and I was dead wrong. Alliances and partnerships change the game overnight ... companies must partner or perish. But defensively backing into partnerships could prove a transparent solution."

Jordan Lewis, *Partnerships for Profit: Structuring and Managing Strategic Alliances*

Then there is the human element. Now we are really talking complicated; culturally varied, economically diverse, and all mixed into some form of organization; with leaders, followers, bureaucracies, policies, practices, norms and communities. Getting dizzy? I am – *but it is all really out there.* Whether you want to consider it all is up to you, but the Value Network includes every bit of this incredible array of "things" ... and more!

Smart quotes

"Partnership comes in various forms: alliances, mergers, content-sharing deals. Call it what you will, everyone is doing it ... [according to] a recent Forrester Research study, 84 percent said the aspect of their business most likely to grow in the next year would be partnerships, far outpacing staffing, technology, content and product offerings."

James Daly

Get smarter about partnerships

So what does this all do to make you smarter about partnerships? First, it will keep you from trivializing them – each of these complicated parts of the Value Network involved the opportunity – no – *the need for partners.* Second, it will help you realize *just how necessary and important doing partnerships right can be.* Third, and perhaps most important of all, you will realize that at the core of it all there is one common denominator in all partnerships – *people* – *partnerships are relationships between people*, then between organizations, companies, etc.

> "Alliances are among people, not just companies … Alliances live through people – this is how all the parts come together."
>
> Jordan Lewis

SMART PEOPLE
TO HAVE ON
YOUR SIDE

People partner first, companies partner to last

Let me say it again! *Partnerships are relationships between people.* Never forget that! The essential success factor in all partnerships depends on one thing above all else – *trust.* Unless partners trust each other at some acceptable level, there will be no meaningful success in any partnership – at least not for long. That trust manifests itself in many different ways, but a few are the most obvious and common.

Fairness and honesty are the first trust-building pieces. Can I trust you to be fair and honest with me? If not, I don't think I want you as my partner. Next comes open communications and information sharing. How many marriages fail because the partners cannot (or do not) communicate openly with each other?

Smart things
to say

Smart partnerships are built on trust, but they operate on shared information!

The corporate equivalence of the open communications is not just to communicate with each other but also to share information openly. It is hard to work together if one of the partners is holding back critical information from the other. Let's stop for a moment and consider how powerful information is today and how much more powerful it will be as a factor in partnerships in the future. Smart partnerships are *built on trust*, but they *operate on shared information*!

> "Another area of huge potential is partnering between employees and departments within the company."
>
> Stephen Dent

SMART PEOPLE
TO HAVE ON
YOUR SIDE

The New Economy – the synergy of information and partnerships

The experts say we are in the information age, the knowledge era, and that the old days of the industrial revolution are gone – fading into the past like the agrarian era before it. I concur. In many respects they are right. The old economy is fading and a new economy is emerging. The percentage of labor in the US still engaged in the production of "things" is dropping steadily. Latest figures have it below 15 percent, and heading toward single digits. But more jobs than ever are being created in the service sector of the economy – and these are heavily information-based and partnership-dependent jobs.

SMART VOICES

> "Trust in organizational strategies and top-management direction is the most critical component in creating a commitment toward a common goal."
>
> Bob Rogers, COO, Development Dimensions International in *The Psychological Contract of Trust*

Like the farming industry decades earlier, technology and productivity have made it possible for fewer people to do more work and create much greater output. There is little doubt that the most vital parts of economies in the US, and all over the world, are growing based on the explosion of information, knowledge, and technology. Call centers and service centers can be located almost anywhere on the globe thanks to partnerships between local communities, communications companies and those who need the call centers.

> "There is only one way to develop an alliance if you expect superior performance: have the implementers be the negotiators."
>
> Jordan Lewis

SMART PEOPLE
TO HAVE ON
YOUR SIDE

Computer programming has become an around-the-clock, around-the-world effort. Less developed countries – like India – are the new programming growth areas for many companies from developed countries in North America and Europe. All of this is due to the synergistic potential of information and partnerships.

As long as we want all of the services and products we use in our daily life, they will have to be supplied somewhere, by someone. In the US, the manufacture of bulky items that are inefficient to ship across oceans will likely continue to be made locally, especially in Mexico, where labor remains much cheaper. More and more products (and now services, too) come from across oceans – often from Asia where labor is even cheaper and more plentiful. This would not have been possible without the partnerships between marketing and importing companies in developed countries, the foreign producers, and liberal information sharing to provide the necessary knowledge quickly and accurately. The ability to transfer know-how across oceans and around the globe via information technology has dramatically enhanced the power of global partnerships.

Q: What is this "synergy," anyway?

A: Synergy occurs when the sum of the parts is greater than the simple numerical total. (i.e. 2 + 2 is not = 4, it is equal to much more than 4! Another way to say it is when the value created is much more than the simple sums of the efforts input.

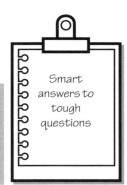

Smart answers to tough questions

SMART VOICES

"It is not the deal *per se* that creates value, but the capacity of two partners to dynamically and creatively maneuver their alliance through a thicket of uncertainties, changing priorities, organizational frictions, and competitive surprises."

Yves Doz and Gary Hamel

Dell Computer is a model of the new generation of demand-pull, mass-customized manufacturers, which relies on (nearby) partners to provide the required components on a JIT (just-in-time) basis. Bulky items like computer monitors don't even need to be moved into the manufacturing plant thanks to third-party logistics partners like FedEx, who can coordinate the simultaneous delivery of the monitor and the rest of the system.

Smart quotes

"IBM allies with Ariba, i2. Trio to focus best of their businesses on Net exchanges"

Headline from *InfoWorld*, March 13, 2000

An auto company like Toyota, with its dedicated, nearby supplier-partners, has provided the best new model for information-intensive partnerships in vehicle production. Toyota relies on suppliers like Johnson Controls for JIT delivery of large pieces of vehicles; thus Toyota becomes, in effect, an information-based systems integrator-assembler. The "secrets" to succeeding at providing manufactured goods or contract services, be they service centers, cellphones or computers are based on four important information and partnership "formulas."

New economic laws and four formulas

The old economic laws that defined wealth in terms of land, labor and capital have been superseded by new wealth-creation factors – information and partnerships. As in the example cited earlier, if I give you a dollar and you

"In our experience, few executives have more than a superficial understanding of what drives the economic and competitive consequences of strategic alliances.

Yves Doz and Gary Hamel

SMART VOICES

give me a dollar, we both still have a dollar. If I give you an idea, and you give me an idea, we each have *two* ideas. The more information is shared, the richer and more valuable it becomes. This is a simple example of the synergy of information and partnership.

Are we using the right technology to be connected as seamlessly and as efficiently as possible to share information with our partners?

KILLER QUESTIONS

Unlike the old determinants of wealth, which were exclusive to their owners and could be shared without being "used up," this new synergy of information grows in value as it is shared and used. This attribute is the basis for the "Four Synergistic Formulas." While these are not mathematical formulas, they are as true as the most logical of the quantitative sciences.

"Being successful in partnerships is a matter of applying a different kind of intelligence."

Stephen M. Dent, *Partnering Intelligence*, Davies-Black 1999

SMART PEOPLE
TO HAVE ON
YOUR SIDE

The critical terms in these formulas are: data, information, insight, knowledge, wisdom, and imagination applied to any product (or business model). Here is how the four synergistic "secret formulas" work.

FOUR SYNERGISTIC FORMULAS

Data + Organization = Information – Most of us are swimming in data, but without a means to organize this data, it provides precious little information. The sheer amount of data often obscures the important information that will allow us to work on the right issues. Burying partners with disorganized data can be deadly!

Information + Insight = Knowledge – Even if a great deal of information is available, only the addition of human insight transforms it into useful knowledge. Insight provides the context and perspectives necessary for partners to understand what customers value and build the relationships that are so important. Partners can contribute valuable new insights!

Knowledge + Experience = Wisdom – Only by combining experience from the successes and failures of the past with the knowledge of the present can we hope to have any true perspective about the future. Downsizing has driven much of the historical experience out of companies and this creates a great risk of repeating past mistakes. Losing such valuable perspective from experienced partners can be equally damaging – and far less evident – until the problems occur.

Wisdom + Imagination = Genius – Rarely do companies or partnerships move to entirely new plateaus of excellence, because they are too invested in preserving and protecting the present successes. When they do make these breakthroughs, they are often handsomely profitable. This requires creative partnerships that blend a special touch – imagination: that almost indescribable mixture of logic and emotion, of science and art – with child-like curiosity and adult determination to weave an entirely new fabric of a business or an industry.

The companies and partnerships that achieve true genius can prosper only if they can collaborate to commercialize it better and faster than competitors. No richer evidence of this exists than the dot-com and e-commerce revolutionaries that were driving the stock market to new heights, only to plummet

> "With trust as a foundation, companies – or groups within a company – can share their know-how to achieve results that exceed the sum of the parts."
>
> Jordan Lewis

SMART PEOPLE
TO HAVE ON
YOUR SIDE

when their imaginative ideas could not be commercialized successfully. Legendary companies like Xerox have failed to commercialize great imaginative ideas. Perhaps Xerox did not follow these *Four Synergistic Formulas.*

The four formulas must be used, with help from partners, to devise winning strategies and the execution to support them – and do it faster than competition. No one owns the exclusive rights to any of these formulas. They are available to everyone. The most important part of their use is embedded in the minds of people, and people are where partnerships are created.

The fifth formula

This brings us to a fifth formula. We are taught in mathematics that a single term is not a formula. Technology alone is nothing. But good people alone are not enough either. The final and fifth formula contains the ultimate success factors in partnering and in business.

- Good Technology + Great People + Sound Strategy + Execution Speed + True Partnerships = Market Dominance

> "Equally novel are the demands partnerships and alliances make on managing a business and its relationships. Executives are used to command ... But in a partnership one cannot command. One can only gain trust."
>
> Peter Drucker

SMART PEOPLE
TO HAVE ON
YOUR SIDE

Whoever has the best-trained, most competent talent, with the right partnerships, and is most able to combine the previous four formulas with this fifth formula will win over all competitors.

SMART PEOPLE
TO HAVE ON
YOUR SIDE

> "There is a night-and-day difference between transactions and alliances. In transactions, contracts spell out everything. … In an alliance, you can't define every detail. Success depends on creatively joining the ideas and energies of the two firms."
>
> Jordan Lewis

Protect the past – and perish!

One of the challenges of partnering is to leave old baggage behind. Too many companies tried partnerships the wrong way in the past and failed. Some of these inevitably led to bad feelings. But that was then and this is now! Times change. People change. Circumstances change.

Clinging to the past, trying to protect its vested interests and political positions without the memories of its mistakes is a sure way to be passed by those who find the way to new and better partnerships. The part of the past that is worthy of protection is the good intentions of those who created partnerships, but even these good intentions must change and evolve over time if they are to survive. Partnerships are not a magic pill. Successful partnerships must grow and change to adapt to new and different challenges. They require persistence, hard work, and commitment. And, if the past was full of problems, it may be hard to let "bygones be bygones," but that is what you must do.

Smart things to say

Whoever picks the best partners wins!

There are some effective assessment tools in upcoming chapters, which will help you figure out why partnerships failed in the past, are faltering in the present, and how to fix them for the future. Corporate icons like Xerox, Kodak, AT&T and many others are in serious decline because their businesses devoted too many resources to protecting the past or perfecting the present, and too few on finding the future.

Perfect the present – and survive?

I bet you think this section is going to encourage you to do better and better at what you are already doing. *Wrong!* I am going to encourage you to do that *while* you look beyond what you are doing now. The challenge of partnerships is the same as most business issues – they can quickly become out of date. That means you can spend only a fraction of your time perfecting the present, because the present will soon become the past – and you know what living in the past will get you – nothing except some gray hairs and wrinkles.

When you try to do this, the problem you will encounter is that your organization, your boss, and probably some of your partners will be obsessed with perfecting the present. It is just human nature. It is seemingly so much safer to perfect what is already in place and working. *Not!* It is the most dangerous thing you can do, because while you are perfecting the present, some competitor is finding the future and will use what they find to beat you.

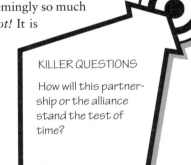

KILLER QUESTIONS

How will this partnership or the alliance stand the test of time?

Well-known companies like Levi's, Kodak, Xerox, Rubbermaid, and even Coke have struggled mightily with the task of perfecting the present only to find competitors had moved on to finding the future and taken large chunks of new market share with them. Levi's lost massive share to Lee (VF Corporation) in the mass market. Kodak was ambushed by Fuji and then by Hewlett-Packard. Ricoh and Canon wounded Xerox. Rubbermaid fell prey to a group of what they called "ankle-biters" led by Sterilite, Manco and many others. Even mighty Coke is struggling, and conceding (non-carbonated beverage) market segments to Pepsi. These once powerful companies took their partners into the declines with them!

SMART VOICES

"If A=B and B=C, then A=C"

"... spend a little time getting to know your customers' customers. If your customer has hitched his wagon to a large, low margin company that has poor long-term prospects, then so have you. This is bad geometry!"

Steve Goubeaux, partner, Visual Marketing Associates

Find the future – and succeed!

What do I mean by this? I mean step back from the press of day-to-day business and think about things for a few minutes (or preferably for a few hours!). What is different today than when your current plans, programs and partnerships were developed? I'd bet a lot is different.

More important, what will be different next week, next month and next year that you just never took time to think about? *Your partners are the critical link to conditions outside your own organization.* Enlist their help to "find the future." Organize a "Partners Finding the Future – Together" conference to discuss what has changed, what is changing and what will

Smart things to say about partnerships

"If we can find partners who help us define the rules of the game and the playing field, we can gain a competitive advantage."

(or may) change in the not-so-distant future. You will be amazed and richly rewarded for doing this.

> "The big challenge in creating the future is not predicting the future, but imagining a future that is plausible – the future that you can create."
>
> Gary Hamel, in "Reinventing Competition," *Executive Excellence*, January 2000

SMART PEOPLE
TO HAVE ON
YOUR SIDE

Use the information gained from this collaborative event to forge new, better and more mutually profitable partnerships. Assess the strengths and weaknesses of your current relationship. Consider the opportunities and threats you see in the market from competitors, from changing conditions, or from your own reliance on past or present technologies when new, better ones are emerging.

The companies that were finding the future just a few short years ago – Dell, Cisco, Sun Microsystems, and America Online cannot rest on past successes. The future is always presenting companies with new challenges and new competition. Only by working in partnerships and alliances, to stay in the forefront, can companies sustain lasting success.

> "Strategic alliances are a logical and timely response to intense and rapid changes in economic activity, technology, and globalization …"
>
> Yves Doz and Gary Hamel

SMART VOICES

Conclusion

I have tried to describe why it is important for you to partner, and briefly what partnership means. I have also briefly covered a few of the critical aspects of partnerships, and touched on the new role of information in partnerships. Now it is time to cover these and many more related topics in depth. There are a lot of smart things to know about partnerships, so let's get into them!

Through the course of this book, I will refer repeatedly to personal experiences and examples of a few companies that, in my opinion, got partnerships right most of the time. (Nobody's perfect!)

- *Huffy Bicycles*, where I spent over 10 years of my career, and enjoyed some wonderful partnerships;

- *Manco* (now a division of Henkel KGAa), where I have been working actively as an advisor and/or board member for 7 years; and

- *Wal*Mart*, which was my largest and most progressive customer-partner for 15 of the last 20 years – dating back to 1980. Now they are many companies' largest customer (at least in North America!).

SMART PEOPLE
TO HAVE ON
YOUR SIDE

"… one must not start out asking 'What do we want to do?' The right question is: 'What do they want to do? What are their objectives? Their values? Their ways of doing things?' Again: these are marketing relationships – and in marketing one starts with the customer rather than with one's own product."

Peter Drucker

I will use familiar examples in the hope that readers can quickly relate to them without a lot of background reading. I may mix the terms *partnerships* and *alliances* from time to time, but don't let that bother you. While most people perceive a difference between a partnership and an alliance, the fundamentals of success in each are quite similar, and the differences can be a matter of definition.

> "Here is a key to alliances: Organizations that collaborate well on the inside have the skills needed for doing so on the outside. The opposite is equally true."
>
> Jordan Lewis

SMART PEOPLE
TO HAVE ON
YOUR SIDE

I will also repeat the "Six Smartest Things to Know about Partnerships" at the start of each chapter. If you take nothing else away from reading this book, I hope you will remember all (or most) of them. You'll do pretty well at partnerships if you do.

Now let's close this chapter with a list of smart partnership priorities. Use these ten priorities as a personal checklist when you first start building partnerships. Having the right priorities will at least get you started in the right direction.

Smart partnership priorities

- *Choice*: choose carefully and wisely – is this an important and valuable partner?

- *Willingness*: are you willing to be a partner, and is your partner?

- *Trust*: does trust already exist or can it be built (or rebuilt)?

- *"CHIPs"*: character, honesty, integrity and principles – must be there – are they?

- *Fit*: strategically, structurally and culturally – can you both make it work?

- *Communication*: and information sharing – will you – and will they?

- *Goals* – are they shared, understood and in a consistent direction?

- *3Rs* – risks, rewards, and resources – are they fairly balanced and adequately understood?

- *Commitment* – does it exist at the top, middle and bottom and across functions in both organizations? Are there "champions" or at least sponsors in both organizations?

- *Measures* – do you both know and agree "what is success" and how you'll know it when you achieve it – and are you both willing to stick to it through good times and bad? Can you imagine the form of partnership this should take?

2
What is a Partnership?

DEFINITIONS AND FUNDAMENTAL TYPES OF PARTNERSHIPS

THE SIX SMARTEST THINGS TO KNOW ABOUT PARTNERSHIPS

No one is good enough to succeed alone.
Whoever chooses the best partners, wins!
Trust is a must – and a two-way street.
There has to be enough in it for both partners.
No support from the top means "no deal."
Power is poison to partnerships.

I believe that there are four or five fundamental partnerships. Some experts would argue that there are many more, but most of them will fit under one of the types I describe here, or in Chapter 4, "Categories of Partnerships." The partnerships I want to concentrate on in this chapter are the ones most business people encounter and must know about.

SMART VOICES

"Before we agree to cooperate, we want to be sure we share a strong feeling that each of us wants to help the other succeed."

Gordon Lankton, president and CEO, Nypro

Partnerships with suppliers

Try making something from nothing. Hard, isn't it? Try making a good product with shoddy materials. This is equally hard if not impossible. Next, try delivering products reliably without reliable deliveries from your suppliers. Impossible, right?

I suspect you are beginning to get my drift. Suppliers are the foundation upon which your business is built. Not since Henry Ford tried to vertically integrate everything that went into the Model T has a major manufacturer of anything complex been successful at supplying everything they need.

In the evolving decades of the US auto industry, it became common for automakers to be quite vertically integrated. Why this evolution occurred is less important than what it led to – an incestuous relationship that is now being disassembled. General Motors spun off its primary parts maker – Delphi; Ford spun off its parts division – Visteon. Both are better companies for having made these moves.

SMART PEOPLE
TO HAVE ON
YOUR SIDE

"… companies that wield purchasing power over their suppliers, like modern Napoleons, get hostility in return. They also receive much less value from those suppliers – in terms of inferior costs, quality, technology, cycles time, and more – than do firms that develop trust in them."

Jordan Lewis, *The Connected Corporation*, The Free Press, 1995

"CEOs will have to manage those partnership relationships to make sure that all of an organization's people – customers, suppliers, and employees – understand what role they play in the vision of the company …"

Peter Drucker, quoted by Verespej, "Only the CEO Can Make Employees Kings," *IndustryWeek*, November 16, 1998

SMART PEOPLE
TO HAVE ON
YOUR SIDE

Chrysler did not have so much dependence on its own parts divisions and in the 1980s and 1990s this actually worked to its advantage. Instead of over-priced and complacent captive parts divisions, Chrysler used the evolving and growing network of auto parts companies that serviced the Japanese imports as well.

The results were lower costs, more innovation, and less fixed overhead for Chrysler in cyclical downturns. Under Tom Stallkamp's leadership, Chrysler was a model supplier partnership (well, for a big auto company – which are heavy-handed partners at best) until DaimlerBenz acquired it.

A company built on partnerships

But let's get back to the importance of supplier partners. There is a great example of just how supplier partnerships can work in building a business. That example is a Cleveland, Ohio company named Manco. Most consumers don't know about Manco, but they use Manco's products regularly. You see, Manco sells Duck© brand tape (or "duct tape" – but don't let Jack Kahl hear you call it that). Manco also sells Duck brand masking tape and carton sealing tape, and bubble wrap, mailing

KILLER QUESTIONS

But, do they really want to be our partner?

envelopes, and shelf liner and much, much more – all through stores like Wal*Mart, Staples, Ace Hardware, Lowe's, OfficeMax, CVS and many others.

KILLER QUESTIONS

Will the partners be able to reconcile and resolve conflicting priorities and concerns?

Surprisingly, in this very competitive marketplace, Manco actually "makes" very little of what it sells. Mostly Manco depends on a few major supplier partners to supply it bulk forms of the items and then Manco "slices and dices" and packages and merchandises the materials for sale in the mass market.

In Manco's case, strong supplier partnerships are not a luxury; they are an absolute necessity. Without its four major supplier partners – Shurtape Technologies for Duck (duct) and masking tapes, Four Pillars for carton sealing tapes, Sealed Air for bubble wrap and mailing envelopes and Vantage for shelf liner – Manco would be out of business! If Jack Kahl, the chairman and CEO who built Manco were writing this, he'd tell you that Manco would never have existed without these partnerships – especially Shurtape and Four Pillars, which go back several decades.

Of course there are other partners that Manco relies on for its supplies, cartons, packaging materials, specialty products, weather-stripping and so forth. But the point is that this company, now a division of Henkel KGAa, the multi-billion DM German company, built its whole business based on its reliance on a few essential supplier partnerships!

SMART VOICES

"When it is possible to fully trust a partner, there is no need to control its behavior. Control comes into play only when trust is not present."

T. K. Das and Bing-Sheng Teng, Baruch College, CUNY, "Between Trust and Control: Developing Confidence in Partner Cooperation in Alliances," Academy of Management Review, 1998

In almost 40 years of business experience, I have seen no better partnerships than the ones between Manco and its key supplier partners. That doesn't mean these relationships are without conflict or free of problems – they are not. It does mean that the belief in partnerships and the bond of Manco with its partners has been strong enough to withstand the forces trying to pull them apart.

KILLER QUESTIONS

Do we both understand the deal we are signing up for?

There are many aspects of supplier partnerships that demand attention, so smart readers must pay heed to them all. First comes the terms of the deal. Unless there is clear, up-front understanding and agreement on the terms of the deal, trouble will be the only constant of the partnership – and it will never be true partnership, because it will have been built on misunderstandings and never lead to a trusting relationship.

Next comes a clear understanding of what it is you are buying. Obvious? Sure! Overlooked? All the time! Clear specifications and well-defined expectations are a necessity. Then comes the price. It will not work the other way around. First decide and agree on what is to be supplied then what it will cost.

> "One of the common problems in partnerships is that the partners fail to quantify their expectations – and over time those expectations change as the people involved change."
>
> Ray Mundy

SMART PEOPLE
TO HAVE ON
YOUR SIDE

As we talk about cost, I must remind readers that there is cost and then there is *cost*. *Cost* is the total cost of what the supplier provides. That includes:

- the freight cost to get the product where it is needed;

- packaging costs to protect it *en route* and make it easier to load, unload, store, handle, etc.;

- marking costs to be sure it is properly identified;

- tariffs or duties if it comes from another country; and

- a host of other costs that are not intrinsic to the product or material itself but must be paid by someone.

Those costs must be somewhere in the price agreed upon! After you have agreed upon what it is, what the terms of the deal are, and what the *cost* is, then comes the issue of consistency – in quality and delivery.

If something is not usable, then nothing else matters. That is why quality is so critical. Quality relies on the specs being accurate and an agreed upon level of conformance to specs, with the associated means of verification. Certification is one popular way of confirming quality. Inspection is the old way of assuring quality – but it just picks out the defects, and doesn't even do that very efficiently. However it is done, quality assurance and the agreed upon method for measuring it is one of the critical factors in a supplier partnership.

If something is not delivered when it is needed, it is of little value. This is why agreement on delivery reliability and speed/flexibility of performance is a critical factor in supplier partnerships. Lead times are usually agreed upon and faster delivery may cost more, and slower delivery may incur penalties – but the best of supplier partnerships use a give and take in this area. If the partnership must resort to "penalties" to make the so-called partners live up to what they agreed to, that is not much of a partnership.

Smart quotes

"Managing the speed of business requires community, tightly forged, with trust that's earned and given."

Jim Kelly, chairman and CEO, UPS, in "Managing the Speed of Business," *Executive Excellence*, January 2000

There are many other issues that can arise in supplier partnerships, but the most critical remaining one deals with all of them – communications and information sharing. How and how well partners communicate and share information is a pretty good barometer of what kind of partnership they have – or don't have! Partners must remember they have to stick together in good times and bad.

While the following insert really belongs a little later in the section on partnerships with employees, it fits well here too. And it is a good lead-in to the other smart things to cover that follow it.

SAM WALTON ON PARTNERSHIPS

In Chapter 17 of his autobiography, Sam Walton cites ten rules that worked for him. After knowing "Mr. Sam" it is not surprising that about half of these rules are about his relationships with his associate partners. I have placed them here because there are few models better than Mr. Sam for being smart about partnerships.

Rule 2: Share your profits with all your associates, and treat them as partners. In turn, they will treat you as a partner ...
Rule 3: Motivate your partners. Money and ownership aren't enough. Constantly, day by day, think of new and more interesting ways to motivate and challenge your partners ...
Rule 4: Communicate everything you possibly can to your partners. The

---

more they know, the more they'll understand. The more they understand, the more they'll care. Once they care, there's no stopping them. If you don't trust your associates to know what's going on, they'll know you don't really consider them partners.

Another statement I heard recently stuck with me on this topic. Without information, how can anyone really take responsibility for something, and with information, how can anyone not take responsibility? Mr. Sam's Rules 5, 6, and 7 are also worthy of listing here, because they are so important to partnerships with employees and associates.

Rule 5: Appreciate everything your associates do for the business ...
Rule 6: Celebrate your successes. Find some humor in your failures. Don't take yourself so seriously. Loosen up and everybody around you will loosen up. Have fun ...
Rule 7: Listen to everybody in your company. And figure out ways to get them talking. The folks on the front lines – the ones who actually talk to the customer – are the only ones who really know what's going on out there. You'd better find out what they know.

Sam Walton with John Huey, *Made in America, My Story*, Doubleday 1992

If it seems like I have cited a lot of Sam Walton here – I have. He created a hugely successful enterprise and left a legacy that endures today, in spite of the detractors and naysayers. Most important, Mr. Sam grew with his business, he kept learning because he was wise enough to surround himself with bright, talented, highly motivated people and then listen to them and let them operate the company.

There are other companies that operate on these kinds of principles too – Manco and Jack Kahl, for example – but they are few. Fewer still have been able to grow as Wal*Mart has and still maintain the essence of the culture – the power of partnership with its associates. Wal*Mart's current president, Tom Coughlin is continuing to lead in the tradition of Sam Walton. Although Wal*Mart and Tom Coughlin now have over 1,000,000 associates worldwide and for Tom to visit them all as Mr. Sam did is nigh impossible, they are still "partners" as far as Tom and Wal*Mart are concerned! Expect continued success at Wal*Mart!

Even customers who gripe about the use of power by some Wal*Mart buyers almost always find an even-handed partnership approach as they move up the organization. Wal*Mart is in business to do what Mr. Sam pledged – to give its customers the best value – always! That puts a lot of pressure on supplier partners – but then those that measure up get a lot of business too. The key is tough but *fair* treatment. That is what such partnerships are based on.

> "Probably a development of greater significance than the advancement in technology is concrete evidence that suppliers and retailers who have developed effective partnership programs are progressing more rapidly than others."
>
> Jack Shewmaker, former Wal*Mart vice-chairman addressing IMRA, circa 1991

The "or else" demand and other bad partnership practices

When times turn bad or economic downturns occur, the temptation to extort savings from supplier-partners is very great. So great, in fact, that most companies try to do just that – and many succeed. When one partner uses power to demand that another partner reach into its pocket and give them money "just because they need it," and they use power to make such a demand, that partnership is poisoned, often forever.

When a supplier is told by a customer, "we a want 5% price decrease immediately – or else [you will lose the business]," the partnership between that supplier and customer will never be the same again. The customer will also never receive the same level of attention, service and special effort again, either! There may be times of extreme hardship when such behavior is "kind of justifiable," but those are rare cases when the customer's very survival is at stake. Even then, the trust basis of the partnership is badly damaged, possibly beyond repair.

Smart things
to say

We have to be honest with our partners – we owe it to them – and it will make us better too.

Leading retailer Home Depot's heavy-handed treatment of its suppliers over the past few years is now coming back to haunt it. Suppliers would rather sell to Lowe's, which is a tough buyer but has not abused relationships as Home Depot did. What did Home Depot do? It simply challenged its incumbent suppliers to offer the best possible deals and then put them up "for bid" with competitors in a so-called "shoot-out" format. The problem was that if a competitor beat the incumbent's deal, the incumbent simply lost the business – with no recourse, no negotiation, nothing – and now, there is no trust either.

There are times when tough dealing is required. There are times when demands must be made. There are also times when a customer-partner *must* take the time and effort to consider the position of its supplier-partner upon making such demands. Otherwise, the "or else" will come back to bite that customer in one way or another, sooner or later. Remember, *"what goes around, comes around."*

What else, how else and the IOU

When a tough customer tries to bully you into a bad deal using the "or else" behavior, one approach you may be able to take is the "what else or how else" response. Pursue the problem as if it were an opportunity in disguise. *If* I can do what you want for you, what else can you do for me to make it more attractive and profitable for me? (After all, he is asking for some of your profit, which you will need to replace somehow.) At least the "what else" question gets their mind thinking in the right direction.

Even if the answer to the "what else" is "nothing else"; you can try coming back with the "how else" question. "How else" can we structure the deal? If the answer to that is "no other way," then you can only try to keep any concession you make visible in the future as a sort of unspoken IOU. Who knows, maybe the buyer will change or the top management will change, and then you can collect on your IOU. Many Home Depot suppliers hope that the new CEO, Bob Nardelli (from GE) will create just such a scenario for "used and abused" suppliers.

Suppliers need to realize that their customers are their "agents" with the eventual end user or consumer. Because of this, the supplier must rely on their customer to keep them aware of competitive conditions, market outlooks, opportunities and challenges and last, but certainly not least, the prevailing pricing trends. Suppliers need to know if they are not competitive, but preferably they need to learn this before they have lost the business. The truth may be painful, but less painful than the alternative. It is the customer's responsibility to make sure suppliers know the "truth" about where they stand. This part of our supplier partnership is now crossing the boundary to the next basic form of partnership – the customer partnership

KILLER QUESTIONS

How well will each partner manage its growing web of alliances without creating conflicts?

Partnerships with customers

Marketing authority Theodore Levitt once wrote, "The purpose of a business is to create and keep a customer," in his classic book *The Marketing Imagination* (The Free Press 1983 and 1986). The wisdom of these words cannot be understated. Without a customer, what is the purpose of a business? Even non-profit organizations, in fact all kinds of organizations, have customers – the end users of what it is they do or provide – whether goods or services.

Smart things
to say

Nothing worthwhile happens
until a sale is made.

Partnerships with customers are possibly the most difficult, yet most important of the partnerships, since a failure here to establish the right kind of relationship ripples back through all of the other partnerships and hinders them. Some customers will attempt to use their power to bully you into the deals that they want. In the short term, you may have no choice but to agree. In the longer term, an abuse of power is poison to partnerships.

In other cases you may be tempted to take advantage of a trusting customer partner, either by charging a higher price or delivering a bit slower, or (heaven forbid!) delivering lower quality. This is a dangerous and unethical thing to do. If caught, any trust will be destroyed, and rebuilding it will be near impossible. Even if not caught, it is simply *wrong*! Don't do it – ever!

KILLER QUESTIONS

Will the pressures
"pull partners
together" or "pull the
partnership apart?"

Another old saying claims, *"the customer is always right."* That is not true. Customers are wrong at times. What is true is, *"the customer is always the customer."* Thus, even when customers are wrong, try to help them. Serving customers is the most powerful and enduring basis upon which to build a business, and to build a partnership.

To use an example, I will return to Manco and specifically to the man who "built" Manco, its recently retired CEO Jack Kahl. Jack will be the first to tell you that "he" did not build Manco – his

SMART VOICES

- The purpose of a business is to create and keep a customer.
- To do that you have to produce and deliver goods and services that people want and value at prices and under conditions that are reasonably attractive relative to those offered by others to a proportion of customers large enough to make those prices and conditions possible.
- To continue to do that, the enterprise must produce revenues in excess of costs in sufficient quantity and with sufficient regularity to attract and hold investors and at least keep abreast and sometimes ahead of competitors.
- No enterprise, no matter how small, can do any of this by mere instinct or accident. It has to clarify its purpose, strategies, and plans and the larger the enterprise, the more important that these be written, clearly communicated and frequently updated by management.
- In all cases there must be an appropriate system of measures, rewards, and controls to assure that what is intended gets done and when that doesn't happen, that corrective action is taken.

Theodore Levitt, *The Marketing Imagination*, The Free Press 1983 and 1986

partners did! But the anecdote I want to use here relates to the motto Jack used for Manco for many years, "Quality + Care = Extraordinary Value."

I will expand more on Jack's philosophy and how it evolved over the years as I use Manco examples in other places, but there are two points I want to make here. Jack was influenced and mentored by Sam Walton, the founder of Wal*Mart. Many of the principles I discuss later are based on my admiration for both of these fine leaders. My earlier book, *The Power of Partnerships* (Blackwell 1994) contains many references to Mr. Sam and his partnership philosophy. Just a few are included here, but now, back to the story of Jack Kahl and Manco.

I recall a meeting at Manco, in which the typical "grousing" about some unreasonable customer's demands was going on. Jack stood up and in his inimitable style, he almost yelled, "stop that!" Then he gave the entire group a brief but impassioned lecture about the importance of customers, and how he would not sit by quietly while anyone "ran them down." He believed in Manco's motto: *Quality + Care = Extraordinary Value.* Few things would set Jack off on an impassioned speech as quickly as someone neglecting the quality of Manco products or the "care" of his customer partners. He remembers how tough life was when he did not have them to complain about!

Customer partnerships are essential to a successful business. Choosing the right customers to build partnerships with is one of the critical decisions of any company. All customers are definitely not equal. Some are more desirable than others are, and the reasons for this vary, from relationships, to the profitability of the mix of products sold, or the ease of the communications with them. Using the Partnership Success Assessment that follows in a later chapter, you can evaluate current or intended customers to see what kind of a partner they are likely to be.

KILLER QUESTIONS

If we don't exist to serve our partners – customers, employees and suppliers, why do we exist?

There are times when you should seriously consider avoiding or even "firing" customers because they can't or won't behave as partners. You may need their sales volume and keep them in a transactional buy-sell relationship for that self-serving reason alone. But don't kid yourself – protect yourself – because these non-partner-like customers are "takers." Their idea of a partnership is "you give and I take." Finally, as Jack Kahl would remind us, once you decide to sell them as your customers, then you are obliged to serve them.

Partnerships with employees and associates

If you are the owner of a business, an executive, manager, professional, or just an employee, you have probably already discovered the importance of partnerships. One of the most rewarding partnerships is with other employees, or "associates" as many of the forward-thinking companies call them. As you might imagine, I really like the term used by Manco. They call them partners! This name came about naturally since Manco was an ESOP (Employee Stock Ownership Partnership) company for many years before its sale to Henkel.

While I was at Huffy Bicycles, we never quite got to the point of changing name from employees to something else, but they were always "Huffy's people" and we knew what that meant! A lot of great companies call people associates and that is a worthy name for employee partners – provided the company acts the way it talks. It is a lot easier to point out the importance of everyone's role in a business if they can all be thought of as "associates" or "partners."

> **Smart quotes**
>
> "What people are craving is meaningful relationships. The same is true for many businesses."
>
> Stephen M. Dent

Fairness is one of the most essential attributes, and perhaps the one I would choose, if forced, to describe the ideal attribute of employee partnerships. I once raised a question with George Plotner, my Human Resources VP, "What is the definition of a fair deal?" He gave me what is probably the best answer I've ever heard, "A deal you'd take either side of." Then he elaborated: "Don't sell a horse you wouldn't buy!" Pretty clear isn't it?

The torn-up social contract

The fancier term for the "deal" between workers and their employer is a "social contract." During the past two decades, this social contract has

SMART PEOPLE
TO HAVE ON
YOUR SIDE

> "To me, the most basic business partnership is the partnership between the company and the people who work there. ...but few companies recognize it as a partnership."
>
> Stephen M. Dent

been torn up and virtually thrown away by many employers (and a few unions, too!). The repeated downsizing, the so-called reengineering programs (many of which were feeble excuses to cut people and load the work on those who remained), destroyed most of the old social contract.

That old social contract was a pretty good one – "a fair day's pay for a fair day's work." Or to put it another way – "do a good job and you'll have a good job." If this sounds like a partnership mentality – it is! As companies merged, consolidating facilities and staffing, there were the inevitable lay-offs, which led to the first tear in the social contract.

Then foreign competition from low-labor-cost countries began invading more developed economies, and more jobs disappeared, creating another tear in the social contract. Employers, no longer able to live up to their end of the bargain in the face of global competition, did the only thing they could – cut people or run away, or both. Employees, however, couldn't run – at least not easily – to the far away places where their old jobs went.

SMART VOICES

> "What might be termed 'the psychological contract of trust' that existed between companies and their employees during my father's working years was blasted out of existence by the business trends of the '70s, '80s, and '90s."
>
> Bob Rogers

> "Don't expect trust between other groups in your firms just because you have been successful together. Those groups may have separate interests and priorities or styles."
>
> Jordan Lewis

SMART PEOPLE TO HAVE ON YOUR SIDE

Next, companies began to systematically mislead or downright lie to employees about what the future might hold for them. Employees who wanted to trust what employers told them were shocked and dismayed when plants closed, workforces were eliminated, and their entire world was turned upside down. Partners tell the truth to partners. Even if the truth is bad news, people have a remarkable ability to accept it and make plans for the worst eventuality. When the truth is distorted or ignored, employees feel betrayed, and rightfully so. The partnership of the social contract, which was largely based on trust, is now damaged beyond repair.

> "The corporate message to tomorrow's managers might well be cast in bronze and hung in the corporate headquarters and read like this:
>
> 'We can't promise you how long we will be in business.'
> 'We can't promise we won't be bought by another company.'
> 'We can't promise there will be room for promotion.'
> 'We can't promise you your job will exist until you reach retirement age.'
> 'We can't promise the money will be available for your pension when you retire.'
> 'We can't expect your undying loyalty, and we're not even sure we want it.'"
>
> Perry Pascarella, noted author and former editor-in-chief of *IndustryWeek* – written circa 1988

Smart quotes

Employees are no longer as loyal to employers because they now realize that the employers cannot or will not be loyal to them (or protect them and their jobs). Thus the only way to rebuild the relationship is based on an open partnership – one of mutual dependence and openly shared information. When companies do this, employees recognize the effort and show appreciation by reciprocity. In these new times, it is not unusual for the more valuable employees to divulge that they are "looking around," or even discuss this with their management, before leaving instead of after!

Despite a couple of decades of misbehavior, companies are now realizing once again that the only sustainable competitive advantages are based upon the talents of their workforces. If these workers are not treated like partners, they soon recognize it and respond accordingly. Sooner rather than later, the best and the brightest people leave for places where they can feel like partners again. Smart companies share liberally – both information and economic rewards – with their employee partners

Smart quotes

"… one of the key aspects of successful alliance management: [is] building trust with your partner, building trust about your partner within your own business, and knowing when you have reached the limits of trust."

Will Mitchell, Professor of Corporate Strategy and International Business, University of Michigan Business School

Special partners, personal or professional

Special partnerships fall into two basic types, professional partnerships and personal partnerships. Each of these will have been a critical factor in most success stories. The smart thing to know is that few people succeed without these special partners' help.

So many different kinds of partnerships fall under this category that the imagination is the only limit. Even competitors occasionally partner with each other temporarily to win out over groups of more fearsome competitors (or to protect their industry from an external threat). Long-term legal and professional advisors, local, state or federal governments, universities, consultants, sales representatives – the list is almost endless.

Usually, however, special influential partners are the most important in this sense. That special personal partner could be a spouse, a trusted friend, or a business partner (in the professional sense). It could also have been a valued consultant, a mentor, a "boss," or it might be someone in your community, club, or church.

> **Smart things to say**
>
> Everybody needs a sounding board – someone who will tell them the whole truth – even if it is ugly.

SUPER SALES REPS – AN EXAMPLE

I know that every successful person I have met has one or more of these special partnerships, which they all value highly and see as instrumental to their success. An example from my personal experience was the partnership forged between my company, Huffy Bicycles and its sales representative firms. During the 1980s and 1990s, Huffy used independent sales reps to sell to all but the largest customers (Kmart and Wal*Mart), and even in the case of those two giants, there was a meaningful role the sales rep-partners could have played. Much of the success we enjoyed was directly attributable to these partners – which I call "super sales reps."

Many companies have since abandoned sales rep firms in favor of customer development teams. The consolidation of retailing has made a different form of integrated sales and marketing teams necessary, and some of the largest retailers (like Wal*Mart) objected to the involvement of a "third-party" in the customer-supplier partnership.

But I am including them in this example because it illustrates how effective sales representatives can be when they are true partners and not just "independent reps." Marshall Associates of Chicago, led by John Kazmer, was one of several superb, professional partners – a sales representative firm. This one sold retailers headquartered in the middle of the US, including Target, Sears, Ace Hardware and many others.

The working relationship between them and Huffy Bicycles in this era was as good as any partnership that can be described. Colman and Hirschmann of New York City, selling customers in the Eastern US, Berman-Purdom serving Toys "R" Us worldwide, Ross-Kerske on the West Coast, and M. J. Daniel Co. of Dallas serving the US military PXs worldwide, were others that fell in this same special partnership model. These were not just company partnerships.

These were relationships we had with the founders and leaders – Austin Marshall, John Kazmer, Tim Scott, Leo Colman, Howard Hirschmann, Ray Himes, Al Berman, Bob Ross, Bob Kerske, and Mike Daniel … and many others whose names could just as easily fill these pages! We fought many battles together – shoulder to shoulder – and won far more than we lost, as partners!

Why was this possible? It was because these relationships had all the requisite elements of successful partnerships:

- The *cultures* of the partner-companies were *well matched*.
- There was *a high level of trust*, reinforced by *extensive two-way information sharing*.
- There were *mutual goals* with *equitably shared risks and rewards*.
- *Commitment* to the partnership existed from the *top to the bottom* of the two organizations.
- *Open, honest communications* allowed issues and *conflicts to surface quickly and be resolved fairly*.
- Finally, there was an element of *mutual need and mutual dependence*, which led to *mutual success!*

Some of these partnerships have changed as time and people and circumstances have changed, but in this era, this is an example of the strongest of special partnerships. Sales reps came under fire in the 1990s and were forced out of many customer-supplier relationships. This is no reason to minimize or misunderstand the valuable contributions they made and valued relationships they created. These were "true partnerships," with quality people.

Other special partnerships

There are many other special partnerships that warrant mentioning. Companies that are supported by their communities are among the most common and effective of these. Professional partnerships between attorneys, accountants, bankers, educators, board members and all sorts of other professional partners enrich the success of companies and organizations everywhere.

In many cases, the most valued special partner is that *personal one* – that person who "tells it like it is" whether you like it or not. Sometimes this is a spouse or a parent. At other times it is a family member, a sibling or a close friend. My wife of 37 years is my most special partner, and my children have become wonderful sounding boards as they have matured and progressed in their business careers and lives.

Church is often the place where unexpectedly productive special partnerships are found. Clergy often have clarity of thought born of more than the cold, hard logic of the business world. To have a Supreme Being as a special partner is a pretty good idea, too. There are a lot of situations where *prayer* – to the "ultimate special partner" – *is one of the smartest things you can do*. Even the toughest agnostics (or self-proclaimed atheists) will surely utter the words "Thank God" or "God help me" more than once in their lives.

Regardless of the nature or the source – these special partnerships are at least as important, if not more important to know about than any of the other partnerships.

SMART PEOPLE
TO HAVE ON
YOUR SIDE

> "Only with joint leadership can you expect joint followership."
>
> Jordan Lewis

Eight essentials for partnership

If you want to have a successful partnership, there is a series of necessary ingredients that must exist. I cover these ingredients in different places, and different ways in the book, so you can choose the approach that seems clearest and most useful to you. To help remember them, I have used eight terms that all start with W to describe them. The eight terms to remember are:

why, which, win-win, will, way, walk, when, who.

I will cover each term briefly to make sure you understand what it means, and how it will relate to material that will be covered in more detail in later chapters.

SMART PEOPLE
TO HAVE ON
YOUR SIDE

> "To create change in organizations, a high degree of trust must be present; without it, no change effort can succeed. The question, of course, is how to establish trust in a compromised and cynical environment."
>
> Bob Rogers

Why

Why partner with anyone at all? This is certainly the starting point. Why not do it all yourself? Henry Ford tried this, as I have already pointed out before. It sort of works, if you have enough resources and a very powerful position in an emerging market. But "going it alone" is not a long-term solution. Everybody and every company need help from someone. No one is good enough at everything to do it alone – at least not for long. Thus the reason for partnering – necessity!

KILLER QUESTIONS

Have we chosen the right partner(s)? Are we sure?

Which

Which of the many potential partners will you choose to partner with? This choice often has more to do with the potential success of the partnership than any other decision. Because of this is it smart to take great care in choosing which companies you will build partnerships with, and which ones you will not.

Win-win

Win-win is by far the best outcome of a partnership. Can the partnership or alliance you are contemplating have a win-win outcome? Everything else will work better and easier if it can. If a win-win outcome is definitely *not* a possibility, you may have chosen "which" partner poorly – go back to the prior step!

Smart quotes

"The three great essentials to achieve anything worthwhile are first, hard work; second, stick-to-itiveness; and third, common sense."

Thomas Edison (inventor)

Will

Will means the will to make it work. Is there a strong will to do this partnership? Often companies and people enter partnerships with a lukewarm commitment to them. Lacking the will to succeed is a strong predictor of future failure. Are there champions in each of the partners who share this will to make it work? If there is not, the alliance will likely fail as soon as obstacles arise.

Smart quotes

"The difference between a successful person and others is not a lack of strength, not a lack of knowledge, but rather a lack of will."

Vince Lombardi (football coach of the Green Bay Packers)

Way

Way is the means to the end – the path to the desired outcome. At times, the best potential partnerships stumble because no one has considered the way to make them work in both of the partners' organizations, structures, processes and cultures. Can the top, bottom, middle, and all across both partner organizations agree on the ways – the sticky details – to make the partnership work? If they can't, there is probably a more fundamental problem at one of the earlier steps.

Smart things to say

Ideas are a dime a dozen. People who work together to put them into action are priceless.

Walk

Walk the talk or walk away? It sounds great to talk about partnerships until the hard details of how they will work are being thrashed out. Then the actions must match the words, or failure is imminent. The first question you must ask is "will we both walk the talk?" The next question comes if the answer to that one is "no." "Are we willing to walk away instead of making a bad deal?" When the feelings turn awkward, or when working arrangements constantly run into problems, it may be better to walk away rather than pretend a partnership is coming together. The failure to "walk the talk" by either of the partners will be evident soon enough – so don't let it get to that point. Stop and reconsider.

> "Simply put, trust means confidence – confidence that others' actions are consistent with their words ..."
>
> Bob Rogers

SMART PEOPLE TO HAVE ON YOUR SIDE

When

When can we get started and start making progress? If the hurdles described in the prior Ws are being overcome, and if the positives are significantly outweighing the concerns, then it is time to get started. The real issues won't surface until you are well into the partnership. Look for them early, but some just won't be apparent until the partnership is further along. If you think this is a good partnership that passes the other Ws, get going with it. Don't be discouraged by obstacles. Obstacles are inevitable and must be overcome by collaborative efforts of the partners.

> "The secret of getting ahead is getting started. The secret of getting started is breaking your complex overwhelming tasks into small manageable tasks, and then starting on the first one."
>
> Mark Twain (humorist and author)

Smart quotes

Who

Who will own the partnership *and* keep it moving *and* be accountable for progress *and* resolve disputes *and* clear obstacles. Don't tell me that these things will just work out – that's baloney! Decide who the partnership champions are, and who the leaders are, and what kind of problems will get run up the organizations for higher management to help resolve, versus which kind will get thrashed out at the working levels. It is best to resolve as much as possible at working levels since there is intimate knowledge about the real nature of the issues. If both partners have wise leadership, it will force this to happen and only get involved if deep-seated problems seem to be cropping up.

Sure-fire failures

Any smart book would take a minute here to tell you about some sure-fire ways to fail at partnerships and alliances. You can probably guess at the most obvious ones by now, but here are a few that experience has proven to be "deadly."

Culture misfit

SMART PEOPLE
TO HAVE ON
YOUR SIDE

When IBM and Apple agreed to do a partnership for systems development two decades ago, it was destined to fail almost from the start. I would be hard pressed to imagine two cultures less compatible than IBM and Apple

"One of the first questions I ask companies that seek help with alliances is why they chose each other."

Jordan Lewis

in the 1980s. Apple – a smallish, entrepreneurial, creative, free-spirited, loosely structured California company and IBM, the immense, buttoned-up, buttoned-down, tightly organized New York industry leader were as different as two companies could be.

One could imagine great complementary synergies from such an "opposites" relationship but such imaginary benefits are just that – imaginary. It seldom, if ever works out because the people, who are at the heart of the two partners, just believe and behave too differently. A more recent example might be the DaimlerChrysler merger. More often, a partnership blending widely different cultures brings out the worst attributes of the two instead of the best.

Hidden agendas

Partnerships are built on trust and mutual benefits. If one of the so-called partners has a hidden agenda, the partnership is doomed from the outset. The hidden agenda won't stay hidden for long. It will be evident in the behaviors and decisions of the partners and as soon as it is exposed, trust will be gone and the partnership doomed.

In some cases there are proponents and opponents of partnerships. These feelings must be recognised and dealt with or they will inevitably damage any partnership efforts. Partnerships often cause a shift in influence, and the formerly influential people may try to hold onto power through a range of "hidden agendas," ranging from subtle pressure to outright sabotage. Discover and deal with this, or don't bother partnering.

Size mismatch

An unfortunate cause of failure is when one partner has very large aspirations and the other has only modest or low aspirations. The obvious parallel

SMART PEOPLE
TO HAVE ON
YOUR SIDE

"As you proceed, explicitly agree that there will be no hidden agendas ... While it is okay to have conflicting objectives, it is not acceptable to be deceptive about your objectives."

Jordan Lewis

to this is where a very large company and a very small one attempt to partner. Size mismatches come in many forms – aspirations, resources, finances, capacity, staffing, etc. A large retailer buying from small supplier partners is one of the most obvious examples of this.

In my model company scenario, Wal*Mart, the world's largest retailer, is the large partner which genuinely wants to develop new, smaller suppliers because they are often the source of successful innovations. The problem is that many of these small suppliers cannot measure up to the demands of a successful sale to Wal*Mart. They have neither the financial resources, nor the capacity. In fact, after encountering this problem many times, Wal*Mart has developed an intensive screening process for new, smaller suppliers. Such a screening protects both prospective partners, so that Wal*Mart does not list and offer an item that is destined to be out of stock all the time. More importantly, the small supplier is not damaged or destroyed by taking on an obligation that is beyond its capability – at least that is one goal of such a process.

Smart quotes

"Mice and elephants can live together, but the mice have to be quick and the elephants have to watch their step."

In decades past, Sears struggled with the same problem during its growth era. Its solution was often to invest in and attempt to control the small supplier, creating a network of semi-captive suppliers. What was a partnership at the outset later became a power-dominated servitude, and ultimately shifted from a competitive advantage to a disadvantage for Sears.

SMART VOICES

"We define partner cooperation as the willingness of a partner firm to pursue mutually compatible interests in the alliance rather than act opportunistically."

Das and Teng

Failure to "walk the talk"

One of the most common and senseless failures in all relationships – and partnerships or alliances are above all relationships – is to say one thing and do another. Nothing destroys trust faster. Nothing tears apart partnerships faster. The sneaky people who think they can get away with it are the worst ones. Of course they don't get away with being "two-faced" for long. Charlatans are exposed. Traitors are banished (or terminated). In partnerships, as in life, your word is your bond – or it's worthless!

The end of the partnership

Very little attention is given to the ending of partnerships when they are being formed. Maybe this is appropriate, and maybe it is not. Few things are so sure-fire that they last forever. Most companies have average life spans of 40–50 years – and if that is the average, then for every one that lives 128 years before its demise (as retailer Montgomery Ward did), there are some early failures. With these early failures of companies are also the end of any partnerships those companies has formed.

But even if the company continues, circumstances change. Industries change. Technology changes. And competitive

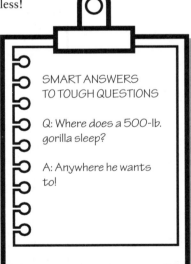

SMART ANSWERS
TO TOUGH QUESTIONS

Q: Where does a 500-lb. gorilla sleep?

A: Anywhere he wants to!

SMART PEOPLE
TO HAVE ON
YOUR SIDE

"There is very little attention given to [how to go about] ending partnerships when they no longer serve the purpose for which they were formed. Market conditions change and the needs from partnerships change too."

Ray Mundy

conditions change. These changes make the need for partnerships different and alter the delicate balance of benefits, risks and rewards. Partnerships have a lot in common with marriages. Euphoria at the start can change to either comfortable satisfaction or irreconcilable differences. I'm not saying that such "marriages" should start with talks of "divorce," but in at least some partnership circumstances, a "pre-nuptial" agreement is a good idea.

SOME QUESTIONS FOR THE END OF A PARTNERSHIP (A PARTIAL LIST)

- How will assets be valued, priced?
- Will there be a prearranged formula and appraisal method?
- Who will own the intellectual property and the rights to it?
- How will assets be divided between partners?
- Will there be a prearranged price formula?
- How will liabilities be divided among partners?
- Who will be responsible for continuing contracts that exist?
- What will happen to people connected to the partnership?
- What will happen to facilities of the partnership?
- Will there be joint announcements, agreed to by both (all) parties?
- Will there be non-compete clauses?
- What country or state laws will govern in the breakup?
- Who will bear the legal costs of ending the partnership?
- Will there be any residual relationship(s)?
- Will there be restrictions and if so, what kind?

In spite of these obvious pitfalls, remember that no one can be good enough at everything. That is why this whole topic of partnerships is so important. In an increasingly complex global environment, a network of partners (a "Value Network") is the key to a successful future. Having said that, let's go on to expand that idea further.

3
Why Build Partnerships?

AN ESSENTIAL PART OF THE VALUE NETWORK

> THE SIX SMARTEST THINGS TO KNOW ABOUT PARTNERSHIPS
>
> No one is good enough to succeed alone.
> Whoever chooses the best partners, wins!
> Trust is a must – and a two-way street.
> There has to be enough in it for both partners.
> No support from the top means "no deal."
> Power is poison to partnerships.

The Value Network™

In a speaking engagement in 1998 the *Value Network* was the name I used to describe a new business concept for the 21st century. In the Value Network, partnerships play a pivotal role, perhaps *the most essential role*! Warning: this chapter of the book is "smart" but it also contains some "heavy ideas." It frames an often clichéd term, partnerships, in the context of a total network that we all know exists, but that we fail to think about most of the time.

A few years ago, writing in the *Wall Street Journal*, Peter Drucker referred to the "Network Society." In his book *The Lexus and the Olive Tree*, Thomas Friedman refers to the "Electronic Herd" and the "Golden Strait-jacket." The names matter less than the fact that there is "something" out there, and whatever we choose to call it, it influences everything else we do. I think the name *Value Network* describes it better than any of the other terms. It is, after all, a global *network* of partnerships which work together to create and deliver *value*!

SMART VOICES

"The answer is to understand that in a world of networks, individuals, companies, communities, consumers, activist groups and governments all have the power to be shapers – to shape human value chains."

Thomas Friedman

Much has been written about "how the Internet changes everything," and how new business concepts are needed because of these changes. The problem is, the Internet doesn't change everything, but it changes so much, that everything else must change. Every company must adjust for the changes driven by the Internet, telecommunications, computing, the information infrastructure revolution and its remarkable rates of technological change. It is impossible to make these adjustments without close-knit partnerships with a large group of constituents, all interacting in a total network context.

Smart things to say

This is a whole new ball game – let's make sure we understand all of the rules.

Fortunately, many of the truths of the old economy remain true. It is these old truths and their relationship with the new truths that we must understand and build upon. *The Value Network is a combination of information, machines and people.* The information (and knowledge) is embedded in the minds of the people and stored and/or transmitted by the machines. The people cannot succeed without the machines, and the machines without the people are worth little. None of them can realize their full potential unless some kind of voluntary partnership is interwoven to make an integrated whole.

"... just as the [Berlin] Wall has fallen down, the good guys and bad guys have gone away – to be replaced by the Web, which is a series of relationships, all increasingly connected with no one really in charge ... The world is setting its own pace, and it's being set by all the people, not one individual."

Thomas Friedman, remarks made at Cleveland (OH, USA) Council on World Affairs, October 4, 2000

SMART VOICES

In the centuries past, wealth was determined by the possession of land, labor or capital – and each was exclusive to its owner. In this new era, information has become the determinant of wealth, and its ownership is non-exclusive. In fact, the more it is shared, the richer and more valuable it becomes to whomever ultimately puts it to productive use. Partnerships simply accelerate the enrichment of information-based knowledge, while the Value Network and its associated machines (and technology in general) spread it around the globe in seconds.

In the 21st century, as in the latter stages of the 20th, value has been the principal determinant of competitive advantage and business success. Who-ever offered the best value won over the competition. But value is a con-stantly shifting thing. To understand it is difficult. To learn, adapt and evolve in order to provide the best value continuously is even more complex and difficult. I devoted an entire book, *The Shape Shifters – Continuous*

SMART VOICES

"I personally see more consolidation: more partnerships, more strategic alliances, and more acquisitions."

Jac Nasser, CEO, Ford Motor Co. in *Fortune*, December 18, 2000

Change for Competitive Advantage (Wiley 1997) to this concept of constantly shifting value and how to capitalize on it.

It was that book and its ideas that made me vitally aware of the existence and power of the Value Network. The key elements of the Value Network are many and varied – but at least these six elements are the most critical, and they fall into three broad "classes." Many of the other parts that make up the Value Network are highlighted in the elements listed below.

The Value Network elements

The concepts

These consist of the *purpose* and *strategy* of the business and the associated elements of its *operational execution*. Within this strategy and execution is the question of who to partner with, and why, and then how to do it. The concepts also include the choices of the *structure*, the *processes*, the *culture* and the *relationships* within and upon which value is created and delivered.

The components

These are made up of the *markets* in which the business operates or which it serves, however defined. Choosing the right *suppliers* and *customers* as partners in those markets and then forging the partnerships necessary to serve those customers better than competitors are the critical keys to success.

The participants

These include aforementioned suppliers and *their suppliers*, customers and *their customers*, plus all of the *employees*, independent *contractors*, members of *corporate governance*, etc. This is the heart of partnerships in the Value Network. Much of it is often called the "supply chain" or "value chain," but it is far more of a complex, non-linear network than it is a simple chain of any sort.

The information and communications infrastructure

This forms the central nervous system interconnecting the preceding parts of the network. This is a big part of what Friedman calls the basis for the "Electronic Herd." Without this central nervous system carrying the information, businesses and partnerships between them will fail and die. The information and communications system is also a synergistic catalyst, which accelerates the reactions that create and deliver value.

The financial investment and physical resources

(land, labor and capital of olden days) that are required to produce or deliver the goods or services by which revenues, net earnings, with positive ROIs or EVAs are created, these are essential to sustain the entire network. Nothing can survive and thrive without enough of the right resources. Special partners are often a rich source of these resources.

The context

The *governmental, economic* and *societal structures* in which the businesses operate and compete are a major part of what Friedman describes as "DOSCapitol" – the "operating system" by which economies and countries control themselves and fuel their growth (or don't).

The environment in which organizations exist and the "operating system" they use determine which kinds of partners they need to survive and prosper. The economies and societies of the world with all of their *governments, practices, laws, rituals, mores,* and uniquely infinite variety are a part of the Value Network's "context."

Smart quotes

"The new economy is global, high-tech, fast-cycle, and networked through e-commerce – four trends that are coming together to change the way we all live and work."

Fred Smith, chairman, president and CEO, FDX (FedEx), in "New Connections," *Executive Excellence* January 2000

Partnerships in the Value Network

How does all this involve partnerships? It involves partnerships totally and throughout, because *The Value Network is the ultimate global partnership system.* Like a galaxy full of solar systems, separate, smaller Value Networks exist all over the world and are part of a giant, global Value Network. Their complexity is now evident by the richness of the *concepts*, the number and magnitude of the *components*, the variety of the *context*, and how *partnerships* are interwoven through and through them all.

Does this overwhelm you? Maybe so! Dare you let it? Emphatically no! Why? Because this is merely a "listing" of all of the interconnected elements among which businesses must currently build and manage partnerships for survival and success. Think of it as a giant Yellow Pages of partnership opportunities and potential. "Let your fingers do the walking," but not through the pages of paper, but on the keyboard of a computer, through the digits and bandwidth of the Internet, around the globe and back!

Q: How can this Value Network work?

A: Here is one short example!

"An importer in Singapore has a large shipment and needs approvals from 18 agencies that handle customers and trade approvals. The trader logs onto TradeNet, a 24/7 Internet-based system developed by the Singapore Trade Development Board, makes the request, and fills out the necessary forms online. The forms are then routed through 18 different agencies simultaneously. The whole permitting process is accomplished online within 15 minutes."

Source: Sandor Boyson and Thomas Corsi, "The Real Time Supply Chain," *Supply Chain Management Review*, January–February 2001

Smart
answers to
tough
questions

That these complex partnership networks are now being recognized in their totality is, in a way, comforting. Horror movies portray the large, multi-tentacled menaces from the depths of the ocean. We are frightened until we finally see them and realize that this is just a "big, tangled up critter" who grew too big for its environment! Something about human nature prefers the known to the unknown, the named to the nameless – and having partners to being alone.

That this Value Network of the millennium we call the 21st century is complex is not the challenge. That has always been so. That nearly all of it involves partnerships is not surprising either. The challenge is the dynamic, turbulent, unpredictable and accelerating rate at which all of these ele-

"If people become reluctant members of your Value Network, eventually they will rebel against it by seeking a different standard."

Thomas Friedman

SMART VOICES

SMART VOICES

"The winners and the losers in the information age will be differentiated by brainpower."

T. J. Rodgers, founder, Cypress Semiconductor

ments are changing. *Start by accepting its existence. Then choose partners wisely and begin untangling the complexity – because you don't want your competitors to do it before you.*

Manco, Henkel and Wal*Mart

To illustrate a real-world example of a Value Network under construction, let me return to my example of Manco, the Cleveland, OH-based company, which is part of Henkel's Adhesives Group. When Manco's leader, Jack Kahl, was considering whether to sell the company to Henkel, he was an astute observer of the globalization of his business. Wal*Mart was Manco's largest and most important customer and it was expanding globally on an aggressive scale. Jack was (as usual) competing with the vaunted 3M for a spot on the shelves of Wal*Mart stores – but now these stores were in new places, like Brazil, Mexico, Europe and Asia.

I recall Jack asking his international VP how many people Manco had in Brazil to serve Wal*Mart. The answer (this was a couple of years ago) was "one – part of the time." Then Jack asked how many people 3M had in Brazil (or South America, near Brazil) to serve Wal*Mart. The answer was "around 3000, give or take a few." That was when Jack decided that going it alone in the coming era of global Value Networks was not going to work – he needed a partner – a big one, and fast. As luck would have it, a mutual friend introduced Jack and Manco to one of the top executives of Henkel, and the rest is history.

In the past few years, Manco's Cleveland-based "Global Business" unit, under the leadership of Jack's son Bill, has introduced Manco's Duck® brand into at least 20 countries. This rapid global roll-out has not been easy, but it certainly was accelerated by Manco's "partnership mentality." Bill Kahl and his Manco partners have enlisted help from their Henkel partners in local and regional affiliates in all of these countries. And, as Peter Drucker said in his "Network Society" article, Manco did not just ask, "what do we want to do?" They asked, "what do they want to do?"

Manco and Henkel are now proudly spreading the Duck® brand of tapes and adhesives to consumer outlets around the world. Not the least of these are in Wal*Mart stores in – yes, Brazil – and in Europe. European retailers are strongly resisting Wal*Mart's invasion into their territory. One of the challenges Henkel faced was if, whether and how to become a partner to Wal*Mart – or an adversary, by allying with old-line European retailers. To Manco and Henkel's credit, a joint management meeting of its senior executives with those of Wal*Mart found a way to begin a partnership. Henkel wisely decided to serve both its loyal, old-line customers and the powerful newcomer, Wal*Mart.

Will the European retailers who are Henkel's long-time customers like this? I doubt it. But most of them will be realistic enough to understand that a global company of Henkel's size and stature (and Manco's strong ties to Wal*Mart) cannot ignore the potential of the world's largest retailer coming into its backyard.

Foreign cultures are ... foreign

These are typical issues the Value Network and the globalization of partnerships are creating all around the world. Different European countries (even regions) have very different cultures. Consider the challenges in large, populous countries like India or China that operate under a different set of rules than Western counterparts. Even different parts of China operate very differently – the coastal areas and provinces surrounding major cities, especially Hong

Kong, operate much more like capitalistic partners. Inland, the further one goes, the stranger it can become. The same could be said for the differences in rural and urban cultures in most countries. This is truly a feature of the Value Network, which can baffle, befuddle and bedevil prospective partnerships.

Here is a story by Mark Graham (*Industry Week*, March 5, 2001) that aptly illustrates the range of good and bad news from globalization of the Value Network.

"In theory, foreigners can come into China independently, without an obligation to find a local partner, but few do, relying on their joint-venture Chinese contacts to oil the communist bureaucratic wheels and sort the workforce chaff from the wheat."

Graham then goes on to describe one joint venture that worked, and the setting for many that fail.

"It is a formula that has worked well for BP Amoco PLC in its far-western venture. The company's $200 million commodity chemical plant in Chongquin [China], built under budget and on time, managed to turn in a $2 million profit during its first year of operation, no mean feat in the boondocks of China."

Just as you might be getting the feeling that applying these partnership principles in strange cultures is not so mystical, I want to use another part of Graham's story to dispel that myth.

"Even with government goodwill and financial sweeteners, joint-venture projects are fraught with potential difficulties and misunderstandings. When Mao-suit-wearing cadres meet MBA-degree-wielding managers, something has to give; outsiders are told that they have to get used to the 'Chinese way,' which often in reality is the 'socialist way,' characterized by intransigence and xenophobia."

You see, the smart thing to know is that among the various parts of the Value Network and in partnering, the culture match (or conflict), is one of the most critical things to understand, deal with and build upon – or avoid as the case may be. Even Manco, as a part of parent Henkel, periodically struggles with the issues of local culture and local autonomy. It is simply difficult for people to put aside long and deeply entrenched beliefs, even if they want to. Never forget that. Mark Graham sums it up pretty well, and I'll use his words.

"And therein lies the rub for manufacturers contemplating a pioneering trip into China's Wild West. The journey may be a rough one; partnering two sets of participants with diametrically opposed attitudes and upbringing is never easy."

The same could be said regardless of the geographical countries involved. Check out the cultures – they are critical to partnership success.

The nodes and the nerds

It's time for a brief word on the topic of people and technology without the daunting complexity of the Value Network as a confusion factor. There is no shortage of technology around. Let's take the well-known example of the supply chain as a case in point.

I wonder why superb supply-chain management is not more common. Certainly, it's not due to a shortage of technical know-how. The "nerds" have seen to that. Today's software and hardware make it possible to manage the supply chain better than ever before. The technology is awesome. Software lets you view the supply chain backward and forward and new improved versions seem to appear as rapidly as wildflowers after a spring rain.

Smart quotes

"Partnering is also driven by network mathematics. On the Web, businesses automatically gain access to the customers of their partner sites. It's the fastest way to spread influence across a network, and, therefore, to build value. Business partnerships have always mattered, but this network effect dramatically increases their importance."

James Daly

So why aren't more companies managing their supply chains better? Concerns about Y2K may have slowed systems development at the end of 1999, but technology isn't the problem any longer. Something else is standing in the way. The weakest link in the most advanced supply chains is not technology, not software or hardware, but at the "nodes" of the network where the people must work together using the technology as they cooperate and collaborate to get results.

Perhaps the term "supply chain" holds a further clue. A chain is only as strong as its weakest link and, while most chains are linear in nature, as I have pointed out before, even the good old supply chain is assuredly non-linear. It is actually a network, not a chain. Make a simple line drawing of yours or one you are familiar with, and you'll see. In a network, the transactions occur between the *links* (those are the lines on a diagram) and the *nodes* (those are the boxes with names in them). The links are the physical moves of material or information. These moves rely on *people at the nodes* who control the flow of both goods and information. The people interactions produce the physical results in the supply chain – whoops! – Value Network.

Usually, the problems inhibiting performance at the nodes can be traced to a lack of trust between people at the nodes and that, ultimately, reduces the performance of the entire network. The lack of trust often stems from past problems. It may also exist due to simple fear or insecurity, perhaps because of conditions within the company or industry. Often it is caused by a lack of leadership and poor communication between groups of people. These people don't work together like partners should because they don't trust each other – for a myriad reasons – and this renders the technology less effective by a huge amount.

Sometimes the mistrust is traceable to untrustworthy leadership. Lack of trust can exist both within a company (or its divisions or departments) and between companies. There is not much difference in the effect on partnerships. In either case, this kind of management is damaging to efforts to improve the performance of the supply chain.

KILLER QUESTIONS

If we have all of the information systems in place, why aren't we using them more effectively?

Victories in the supply chain – and some losses

An old-timer might claim that the supply chain is nothing new ... "just a buzz phrase for the pipeline" or, more broadly, for a new way to do business. Two companies, which have been widely publicized and admired for their supply chain management are Dell Computer and Toyota. Each of these companies have wrung wasted time (and money) out of the supply chain by using what are known as "lean production" principles and tight partnerships with suppliers to accelerate the velocity of material flow to new levels.

Toyota gives Johnson Controls, its supplier of seating, a half-shift (right, just over four hours) of lead time from placing the order to plant delivery, and Johnson completely fabricates seating, stages it in special carriers in finished car production schedule order, *and* delivers the seats (the plants are about half an hour's drive apart). That is material velocity – and that only happens with tightly linked supplier-customer partners.

Dell Computer uses a different approach, coordinating the final delivery of the monitor directly from the producer to the purchaser, without actually handling it in its production plant. Why waste the handling? Just merge the monitor with the system at the appropriate point in the supply chain where the customer's computer is being prepared for shipment (or delivered!).

Other supply chain partners can take over entire pieces of the value creation process. UPS Logistics Group handles the entire process from the time a Ford vehicle rolls off the assembly line until it rolls onto the dealer's lot, and does it in as much as 40 percent less time than Ford used to take. Only with tightly knit partnerships can a process like this be "outsourced" in its entirety.

Smart things
to say

Speed is the ultimate competitive advantage because time is the one truly perishable commodity – once gone, it can never be reclaimed.

General Motors is jumping into the same kind of deal with transportation giant CNF, but using a joint venture with shared ownership, called Vector SCM. It currently takes an average of 13 days for a GM vehicle to reach a dealer, and GM hopes this will cut the time to 8 days. (They will need that, since Toyota has announced its plans to custom build cars for consumers in *five* days!)

Solectron (and competitors Jabil and Flextronics) actually makes the "innards" of many electronic devices from computers to consumer goods, and from circuit boards to cell phones. Solectron is willing to design, procure, produce and warranty its work. This kind of reliance on a third party can only occur when the trust of a partnership is in place.

In its "good days" during the 1990s, Chrysler (now DaimlerChrysler's troubled stepchild) had the highest profitability per vehicle of the US auto companies. According to Professor Jeffrey Dyer in his book *Collaborative Advantage* (Oxford 2000), Chrysler recognized the fact that the fundamental unit of competition was no longer the individual firm but rather the "extended enterprise" – the group of companies that collaborate to produce a finished product. Ford competes with its supplier team against the team of Chrysler and GM (and others!).

Smart quotes

> "Toyota and Chrysler's successes, examined in considerable detail in *Collaborative Advantage*, make a compelling case for the power of partnership in defeating the competition."
>
> "New and Noteworthy," *Soundview Book Summaries*, January 2001

I wonder if DaimlerChrysler recognized that this team was made up of many people who left in the early stages of the merger-acquisition – including the team's leader Tom Stallkamp – who was driven out for telling the German leadership things they did not want to hear! These partnerships can almost work magic, or they can be as fragile as the finest crystal when key people leave and go elsewhere.

Complexity is no excuse

The constant shifting of the shape of value presents many complex issues, but we cannot let this be an obstacle. By choosing partners wisely and building trusting partnerships with them, we will have allies who assist and support our efforts.

SMART VOICES

"Globalization isn't a choice. It's a reality."

Thomas Friedman

The existing names still work. Experts have described parts of the Value Network previously, as the supply chain, value chain, or value web, and these are valid and important subsets. Strategists have coined their own names for parts of the Value Network, as have economists, financial experts and so forth. All agree that partnerships and alliances are essential success factors in these well-defined domains. I do not mean to trivialize or demean the valuable contributions of all such prior fine works. Unfortunately, like the blind men describing the elephant, each perspective is limited by the particular expert's perspective and field of knowledge. Don't get hung up on names. Understand how all the parts interconnect. That is the key.

Not every story describes a glowing success – far from it. This stuff is not easy, or everybody would be doing it. Only a few of the widely publicized and much revered Internet business concepts have shown their viability and, of course, none have been able to show their resilience and longevity – yet. Older business models are showing their age, and creaking under the stress of the Internet era and the phenomenon of prices, which curve down exponentially until they are asymptotic to the zero line. Giving things away free is certainly not a unique idea. Trying to make a profit, and have a positive ROI and EVA doing it is certainly a new, daunting challenge, and one that no one has yet surmounted. The collapse of hundreds of profitless dotcoms is testimony to this fact. When these newborn companies collapsed and disappeared, hundreds of partnerships (and partners) went with them. It's a competitive jungle out there!

The immutable truths

Yet, amidst all of this gut-wrenching turmoil a few truths remain. Value is the name of the determinant of success that packages all of the motives of the purchaser/user into a single complex word. Have the best value and you get the order, make the sale, get the business, or whatever term you prefer. Have the best partners and it is far more likely you'll have the best value.

Now, if you create a network of partners that can produce and deliver that value at a cost less than the price for which you sell it, and do this consistently, then you get a chance to do it again and again. It's called survival. If the price exceeds the cost by enough, it's called success, and if the partnerships are done well, it's a win-win proposition.

Another truth that remains unchanged by the new millennium is that groups of people and their talents, working together as partners, comprise the ultimate competitive advantage. No one organization or company is good enough at everything to go it alone. And no company "owns" its people and partners – they are only rented or shared by employers – and then only for a period of time. If employers can create an environment in which these talented people and partners are motivated to learn from each other, and stick together, then such employers have indeed created tremendous competitive advantage based on a partnership with its employees.

Perhaps the greatest success of Jack Welch during his reign as CEO of GE was that he recognized and capitalized on these facts. GE under Welch didn't just make jet engines, locomotives and financing deals – GE's greatest product was making "really smart people" into its partners in the company

SMART ANSWERS
TO TOUGH QUESTIONS

Q: How many corporate psychologists does it take to change a light bulb?

A: Only one, but the light bulb has to want to change.

Smart things
to say

We are only as good as our
network.

(and banishing the weak ones – just like "natural selection" does in nature!). Then, Welch and his successors provided the next critical ingredient in partnerships and in business – leadership.

The truth is that even with the best of talent and the smartest partners, a company will underachieve without leadership and resources (time, money, technology, etc.). The presence of up-to-date technology doesn't guarantee success. The absence of it does guarantee a dangerous competitive disadvantage for even the most talented of organizations. Thus the technology part of the Value Network and human aspect of partnership power become even more entangled.

Great leadership is hard to find, and expensive – based on the pay packages of leading executives these days. Perhaps this most valued leader is our true Value Network manager! Remember one of the six smartest things to know about partnerships is that without leadership commitment, there is "no deal" – it won't succeed. The most critical resources need no longer be *owned*, but they must be *committed*. They can be borrowed, leased, or even shared in the form of partnerships and alliances – but only in return for some "in-kind" value that the partners want or need – and feel is fair compensation for value given.

Smart things
to say

There is no shortage
of technology – just a shortage
of knowing how to use it and
being willing to change and
learn to do so.

Thus you have it. The Value Network is a multi-faceted, interconnected group of partners (people, organizations, companies, communities, countries, economies, etc.) all interacting in an incredibly complex environment. Change one part and other parts may change as well. Fail to recognize a critical partnership, a link or a node in the network and the traffic stops – as do many of the steps further downstream – unless there are paths around the blockage. Fascinating? Absolutely! Is this a smart thing to know about partnerships? I think so. This concept takes you far beyond where the existing partnership literature has dared to go.

Q: What is the difference between a partnership and an alliance?

A: Here is one viewpoint, and it is a good one.

"In a partnership, the interests are undivided. In an alliance, there is a pact or agreement between the parties to cooperate for a specific purpose and to merge their separate interests and efforts for that common purpose. The pact … establishing their alliance … provides for flexibility. It also recognizes that their interests will differ at times."

Clifford F. Lynch, "Managing the Outsourcing Relationship," *Supply Chain Management Review*, Sept–Oct 2000

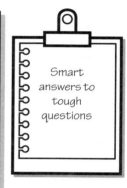

Smart answers to tough questions

Communication can lead to collaboration

Unfortunately, unless there is a great deal of communication across the so-called "boundaries" – both inter-company and intra-company – partner-like collaboration is hindered or blocked entirely. Without this collaboration, the collective wisdom of the businesses cannot be harnessed. People must work together to improve those parts of the Value Network that they influence.

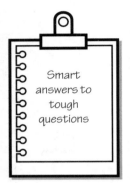

Smart
answers to
tough
questions

Q: Is the trust problem different in dealing between companies, rather than between departments/divisions of one company?

A: Yes, there is a considerable difference between dealing with a lack of trust within a given company and improving the trust in relationships between companies.

The style of the leaders in each of the companies – and how they behave when things go wrong – dramatically influences the trust level in their respective organizations. Trust is damaged when placing blame for failures becomes more important than finding the root causes and resolving them. When going outside the boundaries of the companies, many more issues – like power struggles, conflicting goals and objectives, different or hidden agendas and much more – can undermine trust between the people in the different companies.

But partner-like collaboration is totally a "people thing." It is people working together and collectively utilizing their respective strengths and knowledge. Any collaboration requires extensive sharing. Since everyone views some part of their positional power as being linked to the knowledge and information they control, sharing that knowledge and information represents a risk. "What's in it for me?" they wonder. "And what risk do I take for that reward?"

Overcoming the tendency toward risk avoidance requires trust. Trust that others will use the shared knowledge and information for the good of all parties, and not for some self-serving purpose, like getting ahead or placing blame. Where there has been a legacy of abusing trust or misusing information, knowledge, or power for personal gain at the expense of others, trust is damaged. By now we all know that once trust has been damaged, it is very difficult to repair.

The trust rebuilding process is a slow one – and the effort may be futile as long as the same people remain in their positions. Companies often cause their own problems by establishing an untrusting internal environment. And feelings of mistrust can spread far beyond the boundaries of the company into the other members of its Value Network. Lack of trust then becomes epidemic. Technology and know-how are only as effective as the willingness of people to work together. And trust is the most essential ingredient to building partnerships, which in turn build competitive advantage.

> "Partnership helps organizations build better relationships – which benefits the organization internally and externally."
>
> Stephen M. Dent

SMART PEOPLE
TO HAVE ON
YOUR SIDE

4

Categories of Partnerships

AND THE REASONS FOR THEM

THE SIX SMARTEST THINGS TO KNOW ABOUT PARTNERSHIPS

No one is good enough to succeed alone.
Whoever chooses the best partners, wins!
Trust is a must – and a two-way street.
There has to be enough in it for both partners.
No support from the top means "no deal."
Power is poison to partnerships.

Partnerships are powerful – in many forms

So much of current literature on partnerships deals with specific situations. Even the best business titles speak almost generically of *Partnerships for Profit*, *Alliance Advantage*, *Getting Partnering Right*, *Collaborative Advantage*. And my own first book, *The Power of Partnerships*, is one of a trio along with *The Power of Partnering*, *Power Partnering*. We all seem to agree on one thing. Partnerships are good, powerful, and create advantages that lead to profits.

SMART VOICES

DEFINING THE BEAST: WHAT IS AN ALLIANCE?

- We define a strategic alliance as a cooperative arrangement between two or more companies where:
- A common strategy is developed in unison and a win-win attitude is adopted by all parties.
- The relationship is reciprocal, with partners prepared to share specific strengths with each other, thus lending power of the enterprise.
- A pooling of resources, investment and risks occurs for mutual gain (rather than individual gain).

Source: Booz·Allen & Hamilton, *A Practical Guide to Alliances: Leapfrogging the Learning Curve*, 1993

Most people agree that so-called partnerships and alliances may be classed in a few distinct ways:

- *Partnerships*. Close-knit working relationships between a variety of partners – people, organizations and companies – pursuing common goals in an interdependent manner, but without necessarily sharing (legal) ownership.

- *Alliances*. Less tightly bound arrangements between companies or organizations to achieve strategic or tactical goals based on complementary capabilities, but not shared ownership.

- *Joint ventures*. Legal agreements based on shared commitments and shared rewards and, often, with shared ownership.

- *Mergers and acquisitions.* Transactions in which companies, or parts thereof are bought or sold to re-form the participants' combination of capabilities, markets served, and financial structure.

- *Transactional partnerships.* Usually arm's-length or buy-sell relationships based on contractual agreements, and not usually indicative of a high level of trust, commonality of goals or interdependence outside of the specific transaction involved. (Not really much of a "partnership.")

> "All partnerships don't have to be long-term. Some very successful companies like Dell Computer form partnerships that last as long as the product is offered and the need exists."
>
> Ray Mundy

SMART PEOPLE
TO HAVE ON
YOUR SIDE

Regardless of the form the relationship takes, it is valuable to realize the reason any of these were formed at all. The reasons provide a good platform for planning how to initiate and sustain the partner-like relationship and may indicate which type of relationship will best accomplish the intended purposes (see Table 4.1).

> "The future prosperity of a business depends on its ability to initiate, sustain and profit from interdependent relationships."
>
> Stephen M. Dent

SMART PEOPLE
TO HAVE ON
YOUR SIDE

Table 4.1 Suitability of forms and reasons for partnering

Reason	Form				
	Partnership	Alliance	J-V	M/A	Transaction
Strategic outsourcing	Y	?	?	?	Y
Technology/ proprietary know-how	Y	Y	Y	Y	N
Capacity and/or resources	?	Y	Y	?	?
Skills and/or talent	Y	?	Y	Y	N
Financial and/or economic	?	Y	Y	Y	Y
Special situations	Y	Y	Y	?	?

Y = Probably an effective solution
? = Situation dictates effectiveness
N = Probably not an effective solution

Strategic outsourcing

One of the first reasons for building partnerships is to build greater competitive advantage in "non-core" strategic areas of the business. This is often called strategic outsourcing. Most businesses were born because someone had a better way to meet a customer's needs. Many functions must be performed in any company, but not all are equally critical to the needs of the customer. The most critical ones are "core" to the business. Others (like paying the bills) are necessary, but not "core."

KILLER
QUESTIONS

Do we really understand what is the "core competency" and knowledge of our business now – and for how long that will be core?

Understanding the core competencies that make a business special is the first and most critical step in any decision process on partnering to do strategic outsourcing. If you cannot be the best at something that you must do, it may be wise to outsource it to a partner – unless, of course, it is core to your business. Then you had better "become the best" at it.

Before we go any farther, let's define outsourcing.

Outsourcing is a strategic decision to obtain goods or services from independent organizations outside a company's legal boundaries; to purchase goods or services instead of making or doing them.

KILLER QUESTIONS

Have we considered "insourcing" as fully and fairly as "outsourcing?"

Outsourcing is still most prevalent in administrative and support activities, not in the "value-creating" ones. However, in recent years more companies have formed strategic outsourcing partnerships in what were primary value-creation areas. These new partnerships now result in value-creating

"Some partnerships are formed with the best of intentions but over time the sponsors are transferred or leave one of the companies. Then, the remaining partner's people continue to operate under the 'spirit of the agreement' while the new people at the other partner operate under the 'letter of the law.' This often leads to very different interpretations of what the partnership is all about. A prime example of this is the Saturn (GM) partnership with Ryder Logistics. The Ryder people stayed and the Saturn people changed. The [new] Saturn people had no equity in the understandings of the deal, so they went by the contract – not by the intentions of the original partners. The 'uninformed successors' were simply not aware of the original partnership intentions."

Ray Mundy

SMART PEOPLE TO HAVE ON YOUR SIDE

activities being outsourced to third-party logistics provider partners like UPS, or FedEx, or contract manufacturer partners like Jabil, Flextronics, Solectron and many others. These partners' excellence in their respective specialties has reshaped the old sourcing model.

A ne business concept being widely adopted uses strategic partnerships with certain suppliers to provide the highest level of integrated value – based on close-knit partner linkages and rapid response capabilities. In some cases, well-known companies like Sara Lee have outsourced all manufacturing in favor of becoming a marketer and distributor/systems integrator. This is a role Nike has played almost since its inception. While some of these may turn out to be alliances, joint ventures or simply arm's-length transactions, you simply don't know at the outset. You will begin to see how things are developing as you get further involved. Proceed accordingly, building trust – or safeguards – as the situation warrants.

Strategic outsourcing can be powerful medicine. It is important to understand the benefits, risks and consequences of any strategic outsourcing partnership. These can be far-reaching and have a tremendous impact on your business. The issues that must be considered in such partnerships are numerous, and differ for every situation. Reliance on a partner for critical parts of the value creation process makes partnership decisions even more critical. Here are just a few of the questions to consider when pondering this kind of partnership-based outsourcing.

SMART VOICES

"If a company cannot position itself quickly, it misses important opportunities, whether they are in China or cyberspace."

Yves Doz and Gary Hamel

Strategic issues

- What is "core" to your business?

- What is your true competitive advantage?

- Can you be good enough at everything? (And what are you not good at?)

- Are you willing to share information openly?

- What should you outsource? (Entire products – or just certain components, raw materials, or services?)

Operational issues

- Does your organization have adequate capacity? (Even outsourcing requires planning and management.)

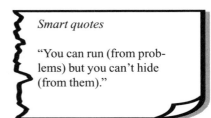

Smart quotes

"You can run (from problems) but you can't hide (from them)."

- What is your ideal facility configuration?

- Should you do "it" the same way across all parts of the company – or differently in different markets, countries, or product lines?

- Is your technology broadly known or is it proprietary?

- Is your demand variable with business cycles or seasonality?

- Who has the best skills and best practices – you or someone you can buy from?

- What are your time frames for decisions required to respond to market/customer needs or to meet competitive threats?

Partnership and structural issues

- Is there a culture match and trust between you and your prospective partners?

- What are your desired terms and duration of the agreement? (What are theirs?)

- Do you want intermediaries involved – and should you?

- Will you use formal contracts or informal agreements? (Putting something in writing is a smart idea, but keep it simple – and no lawyers if you can do it without them!)

- Can you forge true, trusting partnerships, or must it be an arm's-length, buy-sell transaction?

- Should you consider other transaction forms? Are joint ventures, acquisitions, or mergers a better option?

A few words of caution

You can run (from problems) but you can't hide (from them). Make sure that you aren't trying to run from problems that are yours to remedy. If you simply shift them to a vendor, they'll be further removed from your ability to deal with them, but they won't just go away. Outsourcing, like delegation, does not mean abdication. The switching costs from making to buy-

SMART VOICES

"Unfortunately, few managers are prepared for a world in which the boundaries between collaboration and competition are unclear and in which the answer to the questions 'Who are my friends? Who are my enemies?' is not easy and can change overnight."

Yves Doz and Gary Hamel

ing, or vice-versa, may be high. *Don't lose or give away what makes you unique – even to the closest of partners*!

There are many advantages in outsourcing to partners or even to third-party contractors who have special skills, unique knowledge, different resources, or technology that you need not own. Outsourcing the right work to a partner with complementary skills and a compatible culture – and where there is something in it for both partners – is a terrific strategy. The time to be wary is when outsourcing requires sharing too much core know-how of your business.

One of the best ways to decide when and where to use this powerful medicine is to benchmark whoever is best at both the value-added (core) functions and various non-core functions. Then you can decide whether to improve or outsource. But like any powerful medicine, use it with care. Warning: a bad or hasty strategic outsourcing decision can lead to disastrous results.

Why form partnerships – specifically?

One area that is missing from most partnership literature is categorization of the reasons for forming partnerships and alliances. There are many different reasons as there are grains of sand on the beach – but that is not

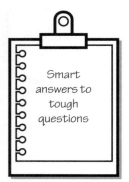

Q: What characterizes strategic alliances, as compared with true partnerships or simpler forms of collaboration?

A: There are many distinguishing characteristics of such "alliances," but these are the most common:

- there is greater uncertainly and ambiguity;
- the manner in which value is created – and how partners capture it – is not predetermined;
- the partner relationship evolves in unpredictable ways;
- today's ally may be tomorrow's rival – or a current rival in another market arena;
- managing the relationship over time is more important than the initial design; and
- initial agreements have less to do with success than with adaptability to change.

Adapted from Yves Doz and Gary Hamel, *Alliance Advantage*, Harvard Business School Press, 1998

helpful in knowing smart things to know about partnerships. What may be helpful is to classify these reasons into some common categories and then consider the characteristics, benefits and pitfalls of each category.

Smart things
to say

Let's think about why we really
want to form this
partnership.

Since each partnership is unique, there is an infinite number of unique categories and reasons for partnerships. Six basic categories may be too few, but there are certainly less than ten fundamental categories, and the more categories I defined, the more they began to overlap. For reasons of simplicity I have chosen the following six categories:

- marketing and/or customer access;

- technology and/or proprietary know-how;

- capacity and/or physical resources;

- skills and/or talent – human resources;

- financial and/or economic resources; and

- special situations.

I'll try to simplify each one to start with, then add the real-world complexities as I go further into what you need to consider in that kind of partnership category.

Marketing and/or customer access

Simply stated, this means forming a partnership to get at customers or markets you just can't seem to penetrate with your normal methods of marketing and selling. These may be industry segments, or far-distant markets. Others may be niches that you can't serve for some other reason – in these cases a partnership may fall into more than one of the categories. There is no limit, except practicality, for how many of these categories a partnership crosses.

Toys "R" Us failed at its first Internet marketing initiatives, so it finally joined forces with amazon.com. This allowed Toys "R" Us to penetrate the Internet shopper markets faster, better and more successfully than they had been able to do alone. Amazon.com

> **Smart things to say**
>
> Let's work on the quality of our partnership efforts first, and then worry about the quantity of partnerships we form.

SMART PEOPLE
TO HAVE ON
YOUR SIDE

"When organizations that have formed partnerships uniquely meet customer needs, they see their market share increase and their customer satisfaction ratings rise."

Stephen M. Dent

got something it wanted too – more traffic on its site and the added credibility of an affiliation with the world's leading toy retailer – along with freedom from inventory or fulfillment headaches.

Another common market access situation involves foreign markets. It is common for companies to form relationships with either distributors or partners when they want to enter markets they are unfamiliar with or ill-equipped to serve. Such an arrangement is both practical and effective. But, this is an area where a common mistake is made.

Companies will partner with someone who is a participant in a "next-door" industry/product segment, and find two things happen. First, they successfully penetrate the foreign market faster than they would have been able to by going in alone. Second, their partner "double-crosses" them and having established the relationships for their products in the foreign market, introduces its own competing products and "steals" the market position it helped establish!

KILLER QUESTIONS

Are there enforceable contracts and rules of law in the country where our partnership will operate? Are we sure of that?

To avoid this requires careful selection of foreign partners and up-front (legally binding – in their country) non-compete agreements. Another protective method is to insist that expatriates participate throughout the process, to build "parent company" relationships with key customers and local market knowledge. No form of protection is foolproof, but to have none is simply being foolish.

Countries like China have become notorious for forming partnerships in which the non-Chinese partner ended up on the outside looking in, and losing its entire stake in the venture. Be sure you understand the applicability of both formal (local) laws and informal cultural norms and business practices as you enter a partnership. What you consider a fair deal may bear no relationship to what the prospective partner thinks is "fair." This may explain why Taiwanese companies (who are true Chinese by heritage) have had much greater success with joint ventures in mainland China than US or European companies.

"Countries like China, for example, select key investors and partners and give them privileged market access while excluding others. In this game, companies cannot play without partners both local and global.

Yves Doz and Gary Hamel

SMART VOICES

Many market-access partnerships are conceived and built based on distribution or sales representation that can rapidly reach a new market segment. Some of these may originate with an OEM sales transaction that evolves into a partnership, then a joint venture, and finally a merger or acquisition. Imagine a skilled producer of lawn fertilizer and herbicides, but who knows little about making application products – spreaders and sprayers. Here is a good candidate for an OEM buy-sell (perhaps with a private label program) to start with. As volume grows, the mutual dependence grows too, and a joint venture is created to expand production capacity. Finally, one of the companies acquires the other or they merge into one entity.

TELEMUNDO AND ARGOS

A win-win partnership?

A late 2000 release announced that Telemundo Network, the US number-two Spanish-language television service, owned by Sony and AT&T's Liberty Media Group, was ready to announce a "wide-ranging, joint-production" deal with Mexico's Argos Communicacion. For Telemundo the deal would ensure a steady supply of fresh programming, and remove the perception that Telemundo is operating at a disadvantage compared with its number-one competitor Univision because of Univision's exclusive production agreement with Televisa, Mexican TV's number one producer.

According to sources, Telemundo will pay Argos $50–70 million for more than 1200 hours of new shows. "This is cheaper for Telemundo and better for us," said Argos Communicacion chief executive Epigmenio Ibarra, who added that anything that Telemundo "passes on" could be sold elsewhere. Under its previous agreement with Azteca, Argos had none of the rights to its programming. "We want to be owners of content," said Mr Ibarra.

Was there something in this deal for both parties? It sure sounds like it. Was this a market access or resource-based partnership? It sounds like a little of each depending on whose side of the table you sit on. This should work, based on these few pieces of information. Both partners get something significant. One gets access to markets and the other gets resources for use in its markets. Win-win partnerships usually work!

Source: Wall Street Journal, October 17, 2000

Technology and/or proprietary know-how

In the prior example of the lawn fertilizer company, there were two motives at work in the basis of the partnership. The spreader producer wanted the market access provided by the fertilizer producer, and the fertilizer producer wanted the durable goods manufacturing know-how of the spreader producer. This means that the category of the partnership is dual – and this is not unusual. More often than not, two partners will have different partnership category needs driving their interest in working together. These complementary needs form the sort of mutual dependence that is good "glue" for keeping a partnership together.

SMART VOICES

"If few firms can now create and deliver products and services on their own, fewer still can control leading-edge technologies."

Yves Doz and Gary Hamel

THE SAD STORY OF SCHWINN

An example of a case of mutual dependence that worked well for most of a decade was that of Schwinn Bicycles and Giant, a Taiwanese bicycle producer. The partnership was formed based on mutual needs. Schwinn needed a producer to replace the bike production from its labor-troubled Chicago plants. Giant needed the know-how to make bikes styled and built to sell into the large and more refined bike dealer market of the US. For several years, both partners played their roles. Schwinn passed on its bike engineering, marketing and styling know-how to Giant. Giant, in turn, learned well and produced good quality bikes at competitive prices for Schwinn dealers in the US – all under the Schwinn brand name.

This decision ultimately led to others, which led to Schwinn's demise. The legendary US bicycle maker violated a cardinal rule of strategic outsourcing – it taught the supplier-partner too much of its core know-how, and then broke the partnership commitment. This partnership flourished through the mid-1980s, until Eddie Schwinn decided to try hedging his bets. But Giant had learned so well that Schwinn feared Giant might sell around them into its US dealer network. Giant did not do this – but Schwinn was concerned about it. Such fears often break up partnerships. In this case Schwinn went (behind Giant's back) across into mainland China to the new industrial city of Shenzhen (not far from Hong Kong) and started another bicycle venture with a private company and the Chinese government.

This confirmed Giant's fears that Schwinn would not be loyal if lower cost producers became available. In retaliation, Giant introduced and marketed its own brand of bikes into the US distribution system – starting with Schwinn dealers! Now both partners had broken trust. The glue of mutual dependence was not strong enough to overcome the fear of betrayal, and the two companies became bitter competitors – to Schwinn's detriment.

As if this were not bad enough, Schwinn made the same mistake again – perhaps out of necessity, but it was no less damaging. Schwinn taught China Bike all about how to build Schwinn quality bikes, then fell prey as China Bike entered the US market on its own. Schwinn's position was only as a minority owner (one-third), but as Schwinn tried to push China Bike into the corner, instead it was Schwinn who got cornered. Who says we learn from experience? Schwinn didn't!

At the time of writing, Schwinn is failing and again for sale, the third time in ten years. Only its brand name and remnants of its once dominant dealer network keep it alive at all.

Capacity and/or resources

One of the major drivers for partnerships is the lack of, or need for, capacity or resources. Strategic outsourcing is one of the forms that this takes. Another is to find a partner with the necessary capacity or resources. What do I mean by capacity and resources? Think about the forms capacity might take – production capacity; labor force capacity; warehousing and storage capacity; computing or communications capacity; the possibilities are endless limited only by the imagination.

Forming partnerships to share capacity may be easier than in many other cases if the use of the capacity is for a non-competing interest. There will inevitably be some form of conflicting competition for the capacity, so the handling of such potential conflicts is an important upfront issue to consider. Often, capacity-sharing partnerships involve intermediaries who resolve conflicts or at least make them less evident by their presence. Contract labor and temporary employment firms are one of the most common third-party partners, as are third-party logistics or transportation firms that permit sharing warehouse space, labor or transportation facilities.

KILLER QUESTIONS

Are we giving away too much of our core know-how to a so-called partner that might use it against us?

Resource-based partnerships go beyond the physical kinds of capacity sharing described above. The most common form of resources provided by a partner is financial, but I consider this a category of its own, and cover it later. Whether the partner is a financier or someone who has the potential access to financial resources, such partnerships can be invaluable. Some examples of financial resource-based partners might be investment banking firms, credit management firms, venture capitalists, or specialists who help companies gain access to equity and investor markets.

As companies grow, their resource needs usually grow at least as fast as the revenue growth – often faster. If a company is successful in gaining large new customers, its capacity to handle the physical business and its ability to finance the new business are critical success factors. The smart thing to do is to search for these kinds of partners before you need them. Create hypothetical situations that represent the upside potential of your business and ask where the capacity or resource constraints would be.

If you do this capacity and resource planning ahead of time, and the big deal becomes a possibility, you will know what you can do to handle it successfully. A common error is to wait until (or after) the potential big deal is at hand, and then scramble for capacity or resources. Similarly, potential partners who might be enthusiastic about the prospects of working with

SMART VOICES

"More than ever, many of the skills and resources essential to a company's future prosperity lie outside the firm's boundaries, and outside management's direct control. In this new world of networks, coalitions and alliances, strategic partnerships are not an option, but a necessity ..."

Yves Doz and Gary Hamel

you will have a chance to get to know and trust you, without the pressure of making a big commitment in a rush.

Skills and/or Talent

Whoever has the best people wins – in sports and in business. But you must have the right talent and skills for the tasks at hand. In sports, having an abundance of talent at one position or skill is more likely harmful than good. An excess of skills in one area creates conflicts, internal competition or strife, and consumes resources needed for talent or skills in other areas. It also does little or nothing to fill shortages of skills or talent in other positions.

Of course, the best solution is to hire the balance of talents and skills needed for the mission and plans of your business. Unfortunately, this is easier to say than to do. Also, conditions change, people come and go, etc. New technology, new customers, new competition, or new constraints can all change the skills and talent needed. When this happens, it is often necessary to find partners with an abundance of the skills and talents needed.

This situation gave birth to the large consulting firms created by the major public accounting firms. The changes in ownership in this field make it dangerous to even name many of these, but Accenture (nee Andersen

Consulting) was built in parallel with Arthur Andersen's accounting practice and grew to exceed its parent in size and independence. The same is true for PriceWaterhouseCoopers and others. Firms like Ross Perot's EDS grew out of the need for talented and skilled support partners in information systems and data center management.

Whether to deal with the now passé Y2K concerns or to capitalize on the explosion of e-commerce, the use of information technology consulting partners is now common. Ariba and CommerceOne are considered critical partners for new B2B exchange operators. Manugistics and i2 are key supply-chain systems partners. Oracle is a strong partner for firms building data warehouses. Telemarketing firms offer large, high-capacity call centers for smaller, niche marketers who wish to sell goods via telephone ordering. Siebel has built a wide array of CRM (customer relationship management) software partnerships. There are literally hundreds of such firms from very large to very small. Be sure to consider the size and culture match when choosing one for a partner.

> SMART VOICES
>
> "The only things you can count on in business are confusion, friction and malperformance."
>
> Peter Drucker

Each of these examples and many more like them are potential partnerships to fill talent or skill needs without the time or inflexibility of hiring regular employees. Just remember that competitors can form similar partnerships, so don't count on these as your primary source of competitive advantage. Partners that are non-exclusive sources of talent and skills may help you achieve your goals, *but if you can buy such help, so can others.*

> "Partnerships encourage creative innovations for improved product design and quality."
>
> Stephen M. Dent

SMART PEOPLE
TO HAVE ON
YOUR SIDE

A more strategic type of partner for skills and talent might be the creative design firm. These too come in all sizes and shapes, and may offer industrial design, graphic design, ideation, marketing services and much more. Large "idea shops" like West Coast-based IDEO or Cleveland, Ohio-based Nottingham, Spirk are creative partners for many leading companies' product development efforts. While these, too, are "for hire," it is more common to form more exclusive types of partnerships with them. Smaller firms, like Dayton, Ohio's Visual Marketing Associates, create collaborative boutique solutions for their partners' creative needs. These more intimate partnerships facilitate free and open sharing of ideas and information, leading to more synergy and closer ties. Such firms normally avoid working for competitors, thus providing a modicum of confidentiality. This type of non-competing-client practice has been in use in the advertising industry for decades, and works fairly well.

SMART VOICES

"In the intensely competitive global arena, companies must identify their skill and competency gaps and fill them rapidly."

Yves Doz and Gary Hamel

A more recently emerging form of skill/talent-based partnership is driven by the rapid globalization of business. Partners from foreign countries can be invaluable resources in providing both the know-how and specific local/cultural knowledge needed to grow in faraway places. It is important to choose such partners carefully since the cultural interpretation of what the terms "exclusive" or "non-competing" may mean in different cultural settings can vary widely. European interpretations are more likely to parallel those of American businesses, while Asian partnership interpretations are much less reliable and require more due diligence. For example, an Asian partner might be very willing to forgo dealing with your competitors, but think nothing of sharing your critical information with a relative in the next city, whose company then sells that knowledge to your competitors!

Finances and/or economics

While I touched on this area under the resource-based partnership topic, it is worthy of its own heading as a driving force for a partnership. In many cases, this is the primary or sole reason for seeking a partner. You simply do not have the necessary financial strength to enter a business or market segment.

In this case, the only choice is to find a "deep-pockets" partner who wants to enter the same market segment, but doesn't have the technical, marketing or product capability to do so. Once again, the term "mutual dependence" comes to mind. Crafting such a partnership requires careful attention to the two partners' aspirations and goals. A few typical US companies that provide such financial partnership resources in return for ownership positions are Harvest Partners (New York), MCM Capital and Bluepoint Capital (Cleveland, OH) and Oaktree Capital (Los Angeles). These firms and many like them will partner with companies and invest in them in return for (usually) a majority ownership position. At times, two or more such firms will share the investment position to amass the necessary resources.

At the outset, all such alliances depend on clear understanding of what each participant will get from it versus what they will put into it. This is as true as ever in the case of a partnership where one partner puts in solely financial resources and the other puts in all the strategic and operating resources. A typical way the financial partner will define its expectations is by agreement on financial measures and the expected operating/financial results – these are usually tied to what its primary lending institutions call "covenants."

Smart quotes

"Show me the money!"

The well-known line from the film *Jerry McGuire*

If the operating partner fails to meet its financial performance commitments, it may also find itself in violation of its covenants, and remedies (or waivers) are necessary. Otherwise, the consequences of non-compliance will result, which can include foreclosure! While this sounds a lot like a "transaction," and is, I have seen many of these where the quality of the relationship defines how rapidly the financial partner "pulls the plug" on the deal. Remember that the financial partner has put both its money and its reputation at stake.

Clearly, the failure of the "operating partner" to live up to its promises is damaging to the relationship. How this happens, how it is communicated, how bad the "miss" is, and how rapidly it can be remedied, have great influence on the behavior of the financial partner. At times, the financial partner will have no choice but to terminate the partnership and/or take drastic steps to protect its financial integrity. In many others, the financial partner introduces "help" in the form of know-how, contacts, turnaround specialists, and occasionally, even more financial resources. At other times, there is a great deal of leeway in how the financial partner may deal with such breaches of partnership agreements or financial commitments.

> Smart things
> to say
>
> Business is a game where the score is kept in money, and winning means we get to play again.

As in all partnerships, the initial understandings of the partners have a lot to do with the strength of the relationship when hardships befall one of the partners. It is unique to the financing partnership that conditions may be less flexible because other, outside parties are connected with the financing. Keep this in mind and don't enter a financing partnership with goals, plans and covenants that are too difficult or impossible to meet. This is a sure way to fail, and to create a climate of mistrust for a long time to come. Remember the old customer service saying here, when dealing with banks or financial partners, it is best to "underpromise and overdeliver."

Special situations

Just as there are always unforeseen situations and outcomes that happen in any business, there are partnership reasons that do not fit any category very well, and I call those special situations. Imagine a situation where two competitors choose to partner for a specific reason that does not compromise their desire to be intensely competitive under normal conditions. Perhaps their partnership has a goal of protecting a local market from outsiders. SMACNA (Sheet Metal and Air Conditioning National Association) is a large national union. Some of its large local members, who are ordinarily competitors in a given major metropolitan area, are attempting to partner in ways that would keep lower-cost competitors from entering their market area.

SMART VOICES

"While alliances can create enormous wealth, they can also become black holes for management time and resources."

Yves Doz and Gary Hamel

A couple of examples from my experience might help you imagine some of these special situation partnerships. The US bike market has always been import sensitive, since bicycles are produced all over the world, and developing countries usually learn to build bikes early in their development, because they provide cheap, efficient transportation.

By the time you read this, very few bicycles will be produced in the US, since Chinese imports have almost taken over the market. This was not always the case. A decade ago, a handful of US bike producers found a special situation where partnering made great sense to them, even though they were ordinarily intense competitors.

This situation was in working together to influence US government regulations on trade, safety, and product liability. It was completely logical and effective for the competing US bike producers to band together to "lobby" against lower duties, and for more reasonable safety compliance rules, and improved regulations on product liability.

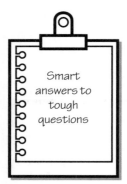

Q: How does this headline event create a partnership or a competitive advantage?

"GM, Ford Combine Web Buying; DaimlerChrysler Joining Venture"

A: It is not clear whether Covisint (as this JV was finally named) creates an advantage for these automakers. It gives them more buying leverage over suppliers, but little advantage over each other. Since Toyota has joined in a limited form and DaimlerChrysler has withdrawn somewhat, only time will tell whether this "marriage of convenience" will make long-term economic sense.

One thing is certain – this is not a "true partnership" between these competitors. It is a transaction-based economic joint venture.

Where common, mutually acceptable goals can be agreed upon, and those goals do not involve the inter-company competition, then this kind of partnership is a good pooling of resources and works well.

A similar situation, again in the bicycle industry, involved competing interests banding together in a partnership – to promote the use of and conditions for bicycles in the US. Industry associations are often groups of competitors who put aside their competitive differences in a common cause to promote their industry's interests. The ski industry in the US has been quite effective in this respect.

SMART VOICES

"In principle, acquisitions are an alternative to strategic alliances. But an acquisition is a blunt tool, often leading one to acquire more, for a higher price, than one needs ... Alliances, therefore, emerged as the vehicle of choice for many companies in both the race for the world and the race for the future."

Yves Doz and Gary Hamel

Other situations often arise where competitors will form alliances in the interest of excluding competitors. When Sun Microsystems began selling Java, it formed alliances with competitors in the interest of pre-empting Microsoft from compromising or limiting the use of Java openly on the Internet. This kind of special situation has become commonplace in computing, telecommunications and other high-tech industries.

The choice of transmission formats for cellular telephones has become a *de facto* partnering process. Sprint chooses CDMA (Code Division Multiplexing), while AT&T chooses TDMA (Time Division Multiplexing), which are incompatible. Other cell phone companies make yet other choices, and the result is that some are forced to "take sides" and become *de facto* partners as a result.

In periods of rapid technological development and turbulent change, such alliances will spring up and then be rendered ineffective, only to spawn new ones. The early days of the Internet had such a proliferation of so-called alliances and partnerships that merely keeping track of them all was nearly impossible. As shakeouts have occurred, many of the alliances and the companies that formed them are now gone and new ones have sprung up to take their place. These special situations are not usually true partnerships but can lead to some interesting joint ventures or even mergers/acquisitions – like AOL and Time Warner!

What the combination of second place or worse contenders in a separate company will do is questionable – except to create an also-ran competitor in which the two owner-partners can squabble over who takes the losses. It is proclaimed as an attempt to rejuvenate "flagging businesses" with well-known brands that never entirely fit the parent companies' portfolios. This one smells like a lose-lose deal, and only meets the needs of P&G and Coke to move these units out of the mainstream of their respective companies – which may be a good enough reason. The phrase *"we felt an alliance would generate significantly more shareholder value*," says that they both want them out of their business portfolios and no one will buy them, so they'll put them together and see how they do.

Coke CEO Doug Daft has been called "Dr Relationship," since repairing severed ties is what Daft has been doing ever since Coke's board put him in charge. Writer Patricia Sellers, in a March 19, 2001 *Fortune* magazine article characterized him this way. "Daft's passion for partnership has led him into strange territory – most notably into a joint venture with Procter & Gamble, announced in February, that pours Coke's juice business (Minute Maid, Fruitopia) and some weak P&G brands, mainly sunny Delight and Pringles chips, into one jointly owned company. Is Doug daft?"

PRINGLES®/SUNNY DELIGHT® AND MINUTE MAID®/HI-C®

A marriage made in mediocrity?

If you have read this far, you are getting smarter about partnerships by the minute. You may see the flaws and problems inherent in this "special situation" partnership announced in early 2001. US consumer goods leader Procter & Gamble and soft drink leader Coca-Cola announced that they would partner to form a third company, which would be owned fifty-fifty between the partners.

This company would market P&G's Pringles® potato chips (a ho-hum performer for years) and Sunny Delight® juice-type drinks, along with Coke's Minute Maid® juice products. This is a big deal, with each partner's brands bringing about $2 billion in US sales, but probably not a good deal. Minute Maid® is a strong, large juice brand, but still a distant no. 2 to PepsiCo's Tropicana®. Pringles® have always been more novelty than mainstream in salty snacks where PepsiCo's Frito-Lay® dominates the field. Sunny Delight® is among many contenders in the "new juice" field established and dominated by Snapple®, Gatorade®, and a host of others.

I don't think Daft is daft – but I do think his beliefs in partnering as a solution for problems led him to this deal. Daft himself says, "Relationships are our lifeblood." He contends that Coke's partnerships (like this one with P&G and another with Nestlé to sell coffee and tea) are good ways for Coke to "outsource" capital-hungry, non-core businesses. The way he puts it makes it clear, *"We don't want to be the snack food company."* Daft even reminded the Coke board recently, *"Our business stands or falls on the success of brand Coca-Cola. Never forget it."*

Unfortunately, many outsiders and some on the board are not so sure this partnership is one they like. They fear that he is trying to "run and hide" from Coke's failures in these non-cola product areas, and at too great a cost. Wall Street analysts think he stands little chance of meeting his professed goals of 15 percent annual earnings growth this way.

The conclusion to all of this will be played out over the next few years. The point of these examples is that partnerships will do many things, but not all of them are so clearly good (or bad) or that everyone will agree on how they'll work out. A consensus of many experts says this one is probably a bad idea, but only time will tell. Win-win partnerships usually win and "lose-lose" partnership deals usually … lose … the question is, which one of these is this deal?

5
The Critical Factors in Any Partnership

TRUST IS THE MUST – BUT NOT THE ONLY ONE

THE SIX SMARTEST THINGS TO KNOW ABOUT PARTNERSHIPS

No one is good enough to succeed alone.
Whoever chooses the best partners, wins!
Trust is a must – and a two-way street.
There has to be enough in it for both partners.
No support from the top means "no deal."
Power is poison to partnerships.

Trust

I could write a whole book about trust and partnerships – but fortunately I do not have to. Someone else already wrote that book – Jordan Lewis – and it is a good one. *Trusted Partners* (The Free Press, 1999) is the name of the book and it is cited frequently throughout this one. It is excellent reading and will go into far more detail and cite more examples than this book can devote to the topic. Having told you this, maybe you don't have time to read another whole book on this topic. That is why I will cover this critical factor in some detail here, because without trust, everything else becomes secondary.

Leading consulting organizations that work with companies and employees on building teamwork and partnerships have also developed some excellent material on the topic of trust. Development Dimensions International (DDI) is just one example of such a company. Much of the time you can do all the necessary things to form partnerships yourself. At other times, or if you want to accelerate the process, it makes sense to seek help from someone like DDI.

SMART PEOPLE
TO HAVE ON
YOUR SIDE

"Mutual trust is a shared belief that you can depend on each other to achieve a common purpose."

Jordan Lewis

The most essential partnership success factor is trust. Without trust, no partnership can succeed for long. But trust between two organizations doesn't just exist in a vacuum. It must be earned, built and maintained over time. The partnering organizations and the people in them may have widely different attitudes about trust.

Some of these people will base their behavior on what has happened in past experiences. If those partnering experiences were good ones, and trust was built and sustained, their attitudes and behaviors are likely to be positive. If prior experiences were unpleasant ones, there is likely to be a prevailing attitude that is untrusting and negative. Behaviors will mirror this attitude. Suspicion, cynicism and outright contempt for new partnership activities are often the product of failed earlier experiences. These feelings represent huge obstacles to building future partnerships.

THE CONDITIONS FOR TRUST

- Priority Mutual Need
- Personal Relationships
- Joint Leaders
- Shared Objectives
- Safeguards
- Commitment
- Adaptable Organizations
- Continuity

Jordan Lewis

Do some homework

Gather as much information as you can about your desired partner(s) and their past experiences. Honestly list all the "issues and obstacles" that you know currently exist. This will only be a partial list, because many exist that you cannot know about – or even imagine. Face the difficult and most awkward ones right upfront. If you don't, they will delay or even prevent the success of the partnership. Only by surfacing these issues and dealing with them openly and above board can a genuine high-trust environment be initiated.

Partnerships must ultimately be built on trust, but you know that trust is hard to earn and easily lost. If you are deemed untrustworthy, you will be considered an undesirable partner. You may not deserve an untrustworthy

SMART VOICES

"Willingly discussing our differences helped us build trust with each other. It increased our shared understandings and by acknowledging our differences, we could more easily deal with them."

Dick Murphy, SeaLand Corp.

reputation, but until you find the source of this perception you can't deal with it. Stories about how you dealt with other partners are often distorted, especially if a former partner is attempting to explain a failed partnership attempt. Rumors spread until they are set right and/or killed by the light of facts and truth.

TRUST BUILDERS AND TRUST BUSTERS

Top 10 trust builders

- Discuss
- Recognize
- Support
- Collaborate
- Disclose
- Value
- Help
- Acknowledge
- Share
- Ask

Top 10 trust busters

- Hide
- Blame
- Defend
- Argue
- Mislead
- Ignore
- Intimidate
- Abdicate
- Punish
- Assume

Source: DDI's *Trust: Strengthening the Foundation*

To get an understanding of how companies feel about trust and a number of other, related factors let's consider some research. The Association for Manufacturing Excellence, in a 1991 US survey, identified a number of characteristics that defined a good customer and ranked them in importance. While this study is now ten years old, people have not changed all that much, so its results are still largely correct.

These characteristics were very similar to what defines a good partnership (since the supplier-customer combination encompasses two of the four partnership legs). Even though technology and negotiation were ranked low in importance (they might not be ranked so low in the tech-savvy 21st century), the most telling point was what type of factors ranked high.

Relationship factors and process factors were rated the most important. Also evident in the responses were strong feelings about trust builders and destroyers. It is evident from this study of the early 1990s and the list of Trust Builders and Busters compiled by DDI that the basics of trust are the same, and do not change much over time.

SMART VOICES

"Though trust is the basis of business partnerships, few of us know how to build it."

Giulio Mazzalupi, president and CEO, Atlas Copco Group

Some of the trust builders were:

- open, honest, timely communication;

- involvement and participation;

- objective feedback and constructive criticism;

- sharing strategic direction; and

- multiyear agreements when justified.

The trust destroyers were often based on behaviors that did not match discussions (not "walking the talk"):

- unreasonable demands and one-way communication;

- talking about quality and service and then buying on price alone;

- decisions made by (higher) authorities not involved with the partnership;

- leveraging one supplier against the other; and

- basing business on price only, not total value.

SMART PEOPLE
TO HAVE ON
YOUR SIDE

"Quality relationships are so fundamental to alliances that their absence is an early indicator of impending trouble. If people who get involved are awkward with one another, you have four options: coach them on the appropriate style, replace them with others, reduce your expectations, or end the discussions."

Jordan Lewis

CHIPs

CHIPs is an acronym I created to help remember four of the key elements necessary for a trust-building relationship: character, honesty, integrity, and principles. While trust is the preeminent condition for partnership success, there are other ingredients that go into a trusting relationship and make it stronger or weaker. Most relationships are built first on trust, but that trust is a result of the CHIPs of the partners.

Character is a combination of the values and the behavior of the individual people who make up the companies forming the partnerships. Perhaps the most important three words to describe the character and values that lead to trusting partnerships are honesty, fairness and integrity.

Honesty means doing what you say and saying what you will do. It is a value that is present whether you are alone or with others. An honest person doesn't try to "get away with things" even if they believe they would not be caught. I like a humorous story to illustrate this. Two truckers are driving a big truck that they know is 11 feet tall, when they come to an underpass marked "Warn-

THE SOUL OF THE HP WAY – DAVID PACKARD AND WILLIAM HEWLETT

"If history is just, it should remember Hewlett for three things. The first is the 'HP Way' that enlightened model of doing business built on trust. Maybe the best thing about the modern corporate world is that it echoes, if often only feebly, the Way. If Dave was the philosopher of the HP Way, Bill was its soul – and the man who implemented it every day … The second is excellence … And finally, there is friendship … Because they trusted each other completely, they could trust their employees, their customers, and even their competitors. Out of that grew a great company and an even greater business philosophy."

Michael S. Malone, editor, Forbes ASAP, in the *Wall Street Journal*, January 16, 2001

ing, 10' 6" Maximum Clearance." One driver says to the other, "let's try it, no one is looking!" Dishonesty is dishonesty whether anyone is looking or not – as they will soon find out while they try to disengage a stuck truck! (Unless, of course the person who labeled the underpass was dishonest too!)

Integrity is like virginity – you either have it or your don't – there is no halfway. Integrity means following your values and beliefs without being swayed by the many temptations and situations that would make it so easy to do something else. There is no negotiation about integrity. People who have it usually shine like beacons in a darkness of marginal behaviors.

Principles are well covered by Stephen Covey in his best-selling book, *7 Habits of Highly Effective People*. In the words of Covey, principles "are deep, fundamental truths" which guide people's behavior. He describes them as the "true north on a compass," not negotiable or changeable. These principles are so fundamental to institutions, associations, and organizations, not just to businesses that they warrant an entire book, which Covey also wrote, entitled *Principle Centered Leadership*.

The presence of CHIPs leads us to fairness. It is easy to claim fairness, but actions speak far louder than words. In a partnership there will be many opportunities to take advantage of the partner. The more trusting the partner is, the more chances for another partner to be unfair and try to gain some short-lived advantage at their partner's expense. When CHIPs are there, fairness is there too.

SMART VOICES

"A fair deal is one you'd take either side of. Don't sell a horse you wouldn't buy."

George Plotner, president, Management Recruiters of Centerville (OH)

To be unfair is to be dishonest. Both are blatant breaches of integrity and show a person of low character and weak or no principles. What is a fair deal? Any deal you would take either side of is a fair deal. Don't ever "doublecross" your partner, because as soon as you do, you have started the undoing of the partnership as certainly as anything else you could do.

A good test of how well you are living up to these standards is whether you could let your partners listen into your conversations about them. If you could, then you are a real partner. If you couldn't, you might not be. This does not mean that partners need to know everything about you or your business – they don't. Just as you don't need to know everything about them and their business. But if you start "bad-mouthing" them with others in your organization, it will not be long before the feeling of negativity spreads and the partnership starts to unravel.

SMART PEOPLE
TO HAVE ON
YOUR SIDE

"A sarcastic comment made by one person I know was, 'You know a partnership isn't working when you start to treat your partner as if they were one of your operating entities." It shouldn't be this way – but it is."

Ray Mundy

Open communications

One of the best tests of partnership effectiveness is a test of the openness of communications and the amount of information sharing that goes on in the partnership. The more freely and openly partner companies share information, the more likely they are to maximize the benefits of the partnership and minimize hidden agendas. Hidden agendas create mistrust, and misinformation. When information is openly shared, such misinformation is exposed along with the perpetrators.

> "*Key principles* (for all human interaction)
>
> - Maintain or enhance self-esteem.
> - Listen and respond with empathy.
> - Ask for help and encourage involvement.
> - Share thoughts, feelings and rationale.
> - Provide support without removing responsibility."
>
> Development Dimensions International

SMART VOICES

Since the purpose of partnerships is to work together on accomplishing whatever goals have been set, a critical factor in doing this is to hold common understandings. Shared information allows all participants to "feed from the same trough" of information. Errors are exposed faster. Disagreements are discovered. Decisions are based on common platforms of fact or at least similar perceptions. Each of these enhances the likelihood of the success of the partnership or alliance.

Another part of open communications is the timeliness. If one partner is working with older information than the other is, they are not "feeding from the same trough," and one is at a disadvantage – perhaps unfairly so – but certainly this will give rise to problems.

Get connected

With the advances in electronic communications, staying in touch and up-to-date is much easier. Since no two partners are likely to be at the same stage of information or communications technology at the exact same time, this also presents a challenge and an opportunity. The challenge is for the less advanced partner to catch up. The opportunity is for the less advanced partner to use the more advanced partner as a resource to catch up faster!

KILLER QUESTIONS

If the partnership reduces costs, who gets the savings?

Rather than go into a technical discussion of the options available, I will only mention then most obvious one – a shared system via either groupware or an intranet/extranet Web site accessible by password access containing information to be shared by partners. Many other older protocols permit limited information sharing via such means as EDI (Electronic Data Interchange), email, faxes, phone conferences, etc. All are potentially useful, but only if the information is timely, accurate and shared openly.

Whatever technology you choose, "getting connected" to a partner is a good idea since it facilitates information sharing which is one of the keys to a successful partnership. Being connected also can minimize the "he said, I said" and "I didn't get your message" kind of gambits that so often pollute partnerships. Avoiding misunderstandings is important. Being connected will help – if it is used properly.

Just as technology has many benefits, there can be some serious drawbacks to using it the wrong way. Email is a common tool that is widely used and often misused. Don't try to negotiate by email. Don't argue by email. Don't say anything you wouldn't say to the person's face. And don't ever write *and send* emails when angry. Store them and re-read them when you are no longer so upset. There is no "undo" on an angry and crudely worded email. There is only the fallout of bad feelings it creates.

SMART PEOPLE TO HAVE ON YOUR SIDE

"The issue of who gets the savings is one of the best indicators of what kind of partnership it is. The original Chrysler SCORE program was an example of one that suppliers bought into. Savings could either be shared equally or the supplier could pass on all the savings to Chrysler in exchange for more business. A win-win deal."

Ray Mundy

SMART PEOPLE
TO HAVE ON
YOUR SIDE

Mutual self-interest

If trust is the foundation of partnerships, what is the motivation for partnering? I usually avoid generalities, but here I feel fairly safe in using one. No one seeks to form a partnership unless it is in his or her self-interest. There has to be something in it for them! Whether there is something in it for the other partners – well, that is their problem! But that's not really true, is it?

KILLER QUESTIONS

What's in it for us, and how does that compare with what's in it for them?

An essential element of human behavior is that we pursue what is in our self-interest. I will discuss some of this further in a later chapter when I talk about Abraham Maslow's work on human behavior. For my purposes here, I want to dwell on why partners choose to work together.

If you have not thought about your motives, do so. Your self-interest is probably served in some way by forming the partnership you are considering. How? A good test of your ability to be a good partner is in Stephen Dent's book *Partnering Intelligence* (Davies-Black, 1999) on pp. 24–25.

He calls it a PQ Assessment, because it helps you measure your "Partnering Quotient." Will you be a good partner? Until you have considered this, it is premature to consider whether your prospective partner will be a good one. I have reproduced the assessment here. For deeper understanding of it, I refer you to Dent's book.

PQ ASSESSMENT

Instructions

- *The PQ Assessment is not a test.* There are no right or wrong answers. You cannot pass or fail. It is a self-assessment that poses statements you might not normally think about and asks you to rank each statement.
- *Rank each statement.* The ranking you give should be based on your own perception of the statement and should reflect how you would react in a normal situation.
- *Choose a context before responding.* Some people say they behave differently at work than at home or with good friends. If you think your behavior depends on the situation, choose the context (such as your work environment or home life) and think of that context when responding to all the statements.
- *Do not ponder too long over a statement.* It is best to go with your first reaction. If you contemplate too long, you may begin to second-guess yourself. Your initial reaction is usually your normal response.
- *The results are for your eyes only.* There is no need to show the results to anyone unless you want to.
- *Be as honest as you can.* The more open you are in responses, the more accurately the PQ Assessment will reflect your true partnering intelligence.

SURVEY (Reprinted with permission)

Answer each with a number from: (1) *strongly agree* to (6) *strongly disagree*.

I believe a person's basic behavior stays the same over time. _____

I like to do familiar tasks. _____

People tell me I'm inclined to be a competitive person. _____

When I'm with other people, I always make sure my needs are met. _____

In general, I like it when everyone follows the rules. _____

I like to depend on myself to get things done. _____

People need to prove I can trust them. _____

I feel uncomfortable sharing my feelings with others. _____

I believe that actions speak louder than words. _____

I get frustrated being on a team. _____

I tend to make decisions about someone based on what s/he did before. ___

I feel very anxious when I'm in a new situation. _____

If I don't win a conflict, I feel upset. _____

When I need to go somewhere, I prefer to depend on myself to get there. ___

I like to have people prove their facts. _____

I believe in keeping my personal life to myself. _____

Past history is a better predictor of events than a future plan. _____

I get very nervous when I meet new people. _____

I prefer to use techniques I've used before to accomplish new tasks. _____

I'd rather give in to another's wishes than argue for my point. _____

I rarely share family information with others. _____

I think it's important to check up on people to make sure they do what they say they'll do. _____

I will give up something important to reach a compromise. _____

I get upset when people tell me something about myself I don't like. _____

I am more interested in actuality than I am in possibilities. _____

I prefer a signed contract to a handshake. _____

I like having my day planned and scheduled and get frustrated when I have to change it. _____

I feel I am more of a private person than one who is outgoing. _____

I would rather be by myself than spend time with other people. _____

In an argument, being right is more important than maintaining the other's dignity. _____

Total score _____

A low PQ score is 30–80, a medium score PQ is 81–130, and a high PQ score is 131–180, and this ranking represents how you view yourself at this moment in time!

For much more information on score interpretation, see Stephen Dent's book, *Partnering Intelligence* Davies-Black 1999.

After all, as they say about friends, "to have a partner, you must be a partner." Are you ready to give something to get something? Why? How much? For what and with whom and for how long? How is your self-interest served? Understand these points and think about them carefully before embarking on a partnership of any kind.

Comparable goals

After you have considered your self-interest and thought about what is in it for you and your partner, then it is time to think about defining success. Without goals, clearly defined and mutually understood, how will you know when – or if – you have achieved what you set out to do? Unless you and your prospective partner have at least generally comparable goals, you are likely to run into trouble sooner rather than later.

Smart quotes

"It is not from the benevolence of the butcher, the brewer or the baker, that we expect our dinner, but from their regard for their own self-interest."

Adam Smith, *Wealth of Nations*, 1776

Defining your goals is critical but this is only half the battle. Since the principle of partnerships is for people to work together toward common or shared goals, it is necessary to know and understand what your partner's goals are too. One of the common pitfalls of partnerships is when partners go into them with widely different goals. If one partner wants to become the dominant global market leader and the other just wants some incremental sales volume, the disconnect between such widely varying goals will either prevent the partnership from succeeding or tear it apart.

Another pitfall is to go into partnerships with poor or naïve understanding of each partner's goals – and that includes your own. Because the goals must be shared and commonly held, an upfront discussion in which both (or all) partners discuss their aspirations is a good idea. From this kind of session, any wide differences in goals can be exposed, and both partners

"We address ourselves not to their humanity but to their self love, and never talk to them of our own necessities, but of their advantages."

Adam Smith, *Wealth of Nations*, 1776

SMART VOICES

"All the partners (vendors, employees and customers) who participate in the process share in the benefits which are created by:

- Working together to establish the requirements
- Creating a partnership based on trust
- Assuring shipment accuracy
- Responding quickly to order requests and delivering on time
- Forecasting customers' needs more accurately
- Allowing customers to do less testing due to consistent product quality
- Reducing inventory
- Eliminating off-quality goods in production
- Allowing customers to respond to their customers' needs more quickly
- Doing the right thing right the first time"

Source: CIBA-GEIGY's brochure, *The Power of Partnerships*

have a chance to move closer together if they choose to do so. This is also a good test to see whether the kind of collaborative compromises that are so necessary in successful partnerships are possible or likely.

Another approach to widely differing aspirations is to consider going into the partnership in stages, where the partners can assess the differences as the working relationship evolves. But do not follow this approach just to avoid discussing sticky issues. *The greatest cause of partnership failures in my experience is when the two partners are not honest about, or fail to discuss, the difficult issues and potential conflicts at the very outset.* Such issues never get easier to resolve later – they only get tougher – and they sure don't go away.

Eras of rapidly changing or developing technology, such as the growth of the Internet from 1995–2000 usually spawn numerous new partnerships, many of which have incompatible goals. These alliances are frequently "marriages of convenience" and "for the time being." A few will lead to longer-term partnerships, alliances, joint ventures or even mergers. Most will be dissolved, or the participants will disappear. The ones that start with known mismatches will almost certainly fail – even if the individual partners don't.

Balanced risks and rewards

Remember the old story about the equity that the chicken and the pig have in being part of a breakfast of eggs and bacon? The chicken is "involved" but the pig is "committed!" When you consider your role in a partnership, think carefully about the relative risks vs. the rewards. I cautioned you earlier about sharing the core know-how that is the essence of your business.

> Smart things to say
>
> If we try to get something for nothing, what we're liable to get is worth nothing.

A caution here relates to the discussions about resources and finances. Often an enthusiastic small supplier decides to jump into the deep water and take on the responsibility of supplying a huge customer. This can be akin to taking a drink of water from a fire hose. All you wanted was a drink of water and you get your head almost blown off!

If a prospective partner is proposing that you take a disproportionate risk compared with the reward you can achieve, you must wonder about that partner's sense of fairness. I've already talked about fairness before, so you know what that means – watch out!

> KILLER QUESTIONS
>
> If they'll do it "for us," will they also do it "to us" and for our competitors?

If there is something about the partnership or alliance that seems almost too good to be true, look more deeply. Anything that seems too good to be true, probably *is* –

or alternatively, is not "true" at all. You can't get something for nothing, so watch out for deals that make such a promise. Chances are what you will get for nothing … *is* nothing!

Smart things
to say

If we choose to dance with a 500lb gorilla, we need to realize that the gorilla will want to lead!

I don't mean to imply that the risks vs. rewards of partnerships or alliances have to be equally balanced. That is almost impossible. What I do mean is that the relative level of what you risk vs. what you stand to gain, when compared with the partner's risk and reward has to pass the test of reasonableness and fairness. If they don't, step back and look for another alternative – either a different partner or a different deal. The same goes for a match in resources required. Big mismatches can lead to big trouble.

I have included a simple Partnership Success Assessment from my earlier book, *The Power of Partnerships*. This assessment can be used for either new or existing partnerships. It should be completed independently by both partners, and perhaps by several different people at each partner.

Once everyone has rated each topic, it is time to sit down together to discuss the ratings. Concentrate on the ones that have either low ratings or where the respective partners' ratings differ widely. Try hard to keep the discussion on a positive tone – after all, you are trying to improve (or fix) the partnership. Discuss what went wrong (or is going wrong) that causes a particular rating to be low – or the partners' perspectives about it to be so different.

PARTNERSHIP SUCCESS ASSESSMENT

Rate each topic from 1 = very poor, 2 = somewhat poor, 3 = average, 4 = somewhat good, 5 = very good

Item		Score
1	Choice of partners (Is this a strategically valuable partner for your business?)	_____
2	Willingness to become a partner (Does this partner desire to become your partner?)	_____
3	Trust (Is there a good level of trust or the possibility of one?)	_____
4	Character and ethics (Has experience proven this exists or can exist?)	_____
5	Strategic intent (Do the aspirations of both partners match or are they compatible?)	_____
6	Culture fit (Do the partners have similar or compatible cultures?)	_____
7	Consistent directions (Is there a consistent direction for partnering efforts – on both parties' behalf?)	_____
8	Common goals and interests (Are the goals and interests of the partners shared fairly equally?)	_____
9	Information sharing (Can both partners feel good about liberal information sharing?)	_____

10	Risks shared fairly (Are the risks to both partners fairly equal?)	_____
11	Rewards shared fairly (Are the rewards and potential gains for both partners fairly equal?)	_____
12	Resources adequately matched (Does the smaller partner have adequate resources to support the larger?)	_____
13	Duration mutually agreed long term (Do the partners agree on a long-term partnership?)	_____
14	Sponsors in top management of both (Is there good top management support at both partners?)	_____
15	Commitment to partnership by both (Is there a fairly broad level of commitment by both partners?)	_____
16	Value given and received (Do both partners have "grossly similar" perceptions of the value the other brings to the partnership?)	_____
17	Rules, policies, and measures (Do these key measures reinforce the desired partnership behavior?)	_____
	Total score	_____

6
Partnerships that Build Competitive Advantage

HOW TO START AND SUSTAIN PARTNERSHIPS, AND HOW THEY GO WRONG

THE SIX SMARTEST THINGS TO KNOW ABOUT PARTNERSHIPS

No one is good enough to succeed alone.
Whoever chooses the best partners, wins!
Trust is a must – and a two-way street.
There has to be enough in it for both partners.
No support from the top means "no deal."
Power is poison to partnerships.

How to initiate partnerships and alliances

Where to start, what to do? OK, by now you are sick of hearing about all the kinds of partnerships and alliances and all the reasons they are great or terrible, work and fail. You want to know how to get started, and what to do – right?

Choose a kind of partnership (who)

The place to get started is to identify a need. Consider the types of partnerships – with customers, suppliers, employees, and special partners. Then look at the categories for partnerships – marketing and/or customer access, technology and/or proprietary know-how, capacity and/or resources, skills and/or talent, financial and/or economic, and special situations.

Choosing one of these "types" or "categories" is a good place to start. But choose carefully, because success is dependent on making a good choice. Then enlist some support from senior management, unless *you are* senior management – then get support (and accurate feedback) from the working levels, which know a lot more about what really happens in the business.

Many great partnerships start at the VP or director level. People in these positions are high enough to have access to, and influence with, top management (and resources) and yet have a realistic perspective of what really goes on at the working level. Starting partnerships at the CEO level is risky because the people feel compelled to go along but may not really believe in the partnerships. They may just be doing it "to please the boss," which is not a good enough reason.

Where to start – organizationally

Starting partnerships lower in an organization – say at the buyer-seller level – is possible but harder. These levels are driven for short-term results and usually spend most of their time in a negotiating "tug-of-war" over details of the deals. Often the ideas for the partnership can originate from the strong relationships that people at this level can build by working together cooperatively over longer periods of time.

But getting the managerial support for such "bottom-up" partnerships is not always as easy as it should be. Why? Because someone at higher managerial levels in one of the two organizations will be suspicious or fear that this is just another negotiating ploy.

Establishing a multilevel partnership

As the partnership progresses, more and more of the dealings will be directly between corresponding functional departments in the partner companies (and not always through the purchasing-sales interface). Culture and language barriers and issues must be proactively addressed. Once this is done, the partnership can proceed to work on the "business" issues.

Building a partnership on a multilevel organizational basis is the key to both supplier partnerships and customer partnerships, although the multilevel people and respective contact points change depending on which type of partnership it is. Multilevel partnerships can also span another level backward into the supply chain and follow exactly the same process – involvement at different organizational levels – but starting high enough to assure solid support until trust is developed.

There must be some sort of top executive partnering (at the VP, president, COO or CEO level) to ensure that the entire organizations of both partners understand the resources, support, and commitment that come from that level. These should involve face-to-face meetings at least twice a year (more or less depending on the maturity and progress of the relationship). These should be "home and home" meetings, held at alternating sites of each partner. Where the distance or cost of transportation is an obstacle, advanced telecommunications such as video-conferencing can help immensely. (Do not forget to schedule meetings with consideration for the partner's time zone and normal workday! Many a horror story has been told about the Japanese top executives who insisted on calling their US managers at 2 a.m. In the US, many Californians must rise before dawn to "attend" a teleconference thoughtlessly scheduled by East Coast counterparts for 8 a.m. –*Eastern Time*!)

The partnership meetings

The partnership meetings must have both private and "public" phases. In the private part, top executives meet alone to openly share their perspectives on how things are going and raise or resolve potentially disruptive issues. This part of the meeting can be held before or after the "public" part. In large, strategically critical partnerships, it may be advisable to split the top executive part into two sessions, one before and one after the main (public) partnership meeting.

The open or "public" part of the meeting involves the functional team members from both partners and focuses on a jointly developed agenda of topics. Minutes from prior meetings (if this is not the first meeting), including progress on agreed actions, are distributed in advance and reviewed for results, and obstacles (so that top management can collaborate to remove obstacles). New opportunities for improvement should be identified, brainstormed, and then moved to the "to do" list – or put on hold for discussion at a future meeting. Difficult issues or problems, such as failings in quality or service by the supplier, poor forecasting, inadequate lead times, or insufficient communication/information from the customer, are all fair game for this discussion.

Refer to the "irritants" list below for a listing of potential problem causes. Someone at a fairly high level (VP of the host partner) should lead this meeting and keep it on track and on agenda. In partnerships that are moving along well, it is ideal to hold a more relaxed "social" event on the evening preceding the actual meeting (a dinner or reception) to allow personal acquaintances to be made and renewed up, down and across both organizations. Many people in top management never meet the working level people (even in their own companies) in this sort of setting. The importance of this type event should not be minimized – it sets the stage for cooperative relations during the partnership meeting.

There are many other dimensions to this multi-level meeting. Some of these are covered elsewhere as they come up. Rather than try to cover too many nuances here, I want to review a couple of other kinds of partnership meetings that have proven effective. There are at least two that warrant specific mention: the *business (team) partner meeting* and the *functional partner meeting*. These team meetings are essential to the customer partnership as well.

The *business partner meeting* consists of mid-to-lower level working management in the functions that do the primary buying or selling and implementation of the agreed upon purchases and sales. This is the closest meeting to the old buy-sell relationship. The meeting and relationship at this level is really where the "heart and soul" of the partnership lives.

KEY IRRITANTS FROM THE CUSTOMER'S VIEWPOINT:

- Stockouts and late or poor delivery.
- Backorders and long reorder cycles.
- Inadequate communication or poor information.
- Confusing or rapidly changing terms and allowances.
- Unrelated or unclear marketing campaigns.
- Frequent personnel changes in sales representatives or account managers.
- Incomplete or poorly thought-out promotions and plans.
- Inadequate lead times on promotion plans.
- Inaccessibility to supplier management.
- Inexplicable policies (at least by the sales representatives).
- Billing disagreements.
- New product introductions or major product line changes with too little advance notice.
- Decentralized and often autonomous multi-division structures where several sales representatives from the same company sell closely related but different products to the same buyer, with differing terms, programs, and so on.

In the bike business while I was at Huffy, we had a multifunctional, middle managers team that named themselves the Pro-TQ team (shorthand for Procurement-Total Quality). At Manco, more recently, a mid-level SQP team (Supplier Quality Partnerships) was formed. People on these teams were the foremost drivers of the whole partnership process.

That is why partnership meetings should occur frequently. They can be held at any convenient location (even around trade shows) and should be directed primarily at meeting the ongoing needs of doing business with each other – a supplier serving the customer. All sorts of routine matters are handled here – forecasting, planning, general business condition adjustments, operating misunderstandings, error correction, problem identifica-

KEY IRRITANTS FROM THE SUPPLIER'S VIEWPOINT:

- Confusing or complicated scheduling of appointments and meetings with buyers.
- Buying decisions attributed to anonymous sources such as "the committee" or simply "they."
- Execution of delivery, setup, display, or promotion different from what was agreed upon.
- Sudden changes in inventory needs – cutbacks or cancellations or unexpected surges in demand – with little or no advance notice.
- Failure to keep planned meeting schedules or delaying meetings inexplicably for hours.
- Sudden or major strategic direction changes.
- Last-minute cancellation of promotions that had been organized at great expense and for which inventory has already been committed.
- Frequent buying staff changes or changes in the mix of assigned duties.
- Inaccessible senior management.
- Billing disputes and deductions.

John L. Mariotti, *The Power of Partnerships*, Blackwell, 1996

tion (and resolution, if possible), new product introduction, quality or cost improvement progress, and so forth. More important, the partnership momentum is sustained, and many issues are dealt with before they can disrupt the partnership. Other working levels and parts of the two organizations actually do much of the work, but this team is the "engine."

If there are relationships with partners across multiple parts of your organization, you can ask them for their input too, or invite them into the partnership meetings on an "as needed" basis. The success of the partnership will ultimately require support from many departments beyond the one originating the idea. If purchasing or sales is the initiator, then receiving, shipping, accounts payable or receivable, and even engineering or marketing may have useful input. This also helps head off any later confrontations about unknown or serious (unrealized) obstacles – I call them "landmines" – that could "blow up" the partnership effort.

Beware of old mines ("BOOM!")

All companies have buried "landmines" – old problems that were never satisfactorily resolved, with the remains of hurt feelings, bitterness or outright dislike for a potential partner or type of partnership solution. For example, if a partner "stole" valuable technology and turned it against them, a company will have some "landmine" type of reservations about entering a technology-sharing role in a new partnership. If failure to deliver at a pivotal point cost your company a key customer, an outsourcing or capacity-based partnership will meet "landmine" type of opposition from the people in sales.

SMART VOICES

"For partnerships to succeed they must be embraced, developed and continue with trust at the working level with support throughout the management hierarchy all the way to the top."

Bill Lake, president, Royal Medica USA

Categories (why)

Once a good chance for a partnership has been identified, it is time to carefully consider the reasons why. The categories of partnerships describe broad reasons and most cases will fit in one of these categories. When there are reasons from more than one category, that is an indication that the partnership is even more desirable, if the questions about choosing – issues like compatibility of culture, character, common goals and collaborative motives – can be satisfied.

Now you have considered who to partner with, and why you might find that desirable. Look in the mirror and ask if this potential partner would reach similar conclusions. Try to understand how the partner would approach all the same questions you just went through. If the answers (honestly – no point in kidding yourself) are favorable, you are ready for the next step.

Forms (how)

Think about the possible forms of relationship that you might use to initiate this partnership. You may already have the arm's-length transactional one in place. Can you find a form that both of you would probably feel fits your mutual needs. Remember, for every reason you want to enter a partnership, your partner must have one. For each concern you have, they also have one of those too!

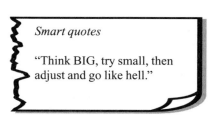

Smart quotes

"Think BIG, try small, then adjust and go like hell."

Timing (when)

If you have considered all of these factors, then the question of timing and how to "tiptoe" into such a relationship is ready to be discussed. Most businesses have seasonality or cyclicality, and entering new partnerships is easier at one time of year or point in the cycle than another. I used the term "tiptoe" in because I wouldn't advise anyone to "jump in" to a new partnership in a big way, without trying it out in a smaller way at first.

SMART VOICES

"He who would learn to fly one day must first learn to stand and walk and run and climb and dance; one cannot fly into flying."

Nietzsche

Certainly, some partnerships will involve commitments that make gradual entry difficult or impossible. The purchase of major tooling and equipment or the construction of plants/buildings or the launch of major advertising campaigns, and financial equity offerings are such large events that "tiptoeing in" may be impossible. But I still believe the prudent thing to do is to "Think BIG, but try small" – then adjust and move forward – rapidly.

Smart quotes

"In theory there is no difference between theory and practice, but in practice there is a lot of difference."

The best advice I can give on timing is "make haste carefully." This means move as fast as you can, but don't take foolish risks or ask your partner to do so either. Assuming the partnership benefits both of you, moving forward promptly makes economic sense. It also makes psychological sense to move while there is still enthusiastic support for the partnership. Time can be an enemy. If a relationship stalls and drags on during the implementation, there is a much greater risk of failure from many reasons – changes of people, changing priorities, market conditions, competitive reaction (competitors will find out – sooner than you want them to), alternative uses for resources, and so forth. So the thing to remember, is "if it's worth doing, it's worth doing right – and it's worth doing *now* – not later on!"

The partnership agreement

Partnerships are actually legal entities. So, do you need a partnership agreement? In many cases the answer is "yes!" But what about all this talk about trust? Doesn't that relieve the need for written agreements? In this case the answer is "no!"

While partnerships usually fail if trust is not present, there are a lot of little irritants, and some big ones that will rear their ugly head if there is nothing written about how partners will work together. Writing a common sense partnership agreement is a good idea – a *smart thing to do*!

SMART VOICES

"Managers cannot be ordered to trust their partners, particularly when those partners are potential rivals."

Yves Doz and Gary Hamel

You can use your agreement to anticipate and plan for many of the eventualities that will come up as you move ahead. You can also use it to raise those sticky issues that are too often glossed over in the beginning, only to become bigger and stickier once you are underway.

What happens if one of the partners wants out? Where do the assets of the partnership go? What happens to the liabilities? Does one of you financially "buy out" the other one – and how is the price determined? How would the proceeds of a sell-out be distributed? There are hundreds of questions like these.

The answers to these and many other questions will be a lot easier to agree on before there is a lot of time, effort and money invested in the partnership. If you don't think about this stuff early, you will probably trip over some of it later on.

Smart things to say

Writing down what we agreed upon is a good way to help the corporate memory recall what it was – and make sure we actually do agree.

There is a great book called, appropriately enough, *The Partnership Book* (www.Nolo.com) that describes all about how to structure partnerships, write the agreements and consider the issues. If you are considering a "legal" partnership, you need "legal" advice – and this book is written by a group of

SMART VOICES	"Our advice is to keep the lawyers and corporate staff away from the negotiating table until most elements are worked out by line managers." Source: Booz·Allen and Hamilton, *A Practical Guide to Alliances: Leapfrogging the Learning Curve,* 1993

lawyers. As they put it "A partnership agreement is not something you whip up between the soup and the salad." Here are a few points you should know about in this area (all are covered in lots of detail in *The Partnership Book*).

Forms of businesses

There are five common forms of business ownership (in the US at least – other countries' laws and business forms vary widely – check your country's laws before acting!):

- partnership;

- sole proprietorship;

- corporation;

- limited liability company; and

- limited partnership.

A partnership is defined as a business owned by two or more people. Each partner can perform all of the actions required to operate the business: making decisions, hiring people, spending money, borrowing money, etc. Each partner is personally liable for *all* of the debts incurred by the partnership

– and that includes those that another partner incurred! If your partnership has a claim against it and its assets are not sufficient to fulfill that claim, your personal assets can be taken to pay for business debts! Before you ask – yes, your partner can make agreements and create obligations that you are liable for!

This is why most of the partnerships I am talking about in this book are between people who are part of business entities that have considered these liability issues and taken care of them – i.e. corporations, LLCs, etc.

Q: You mean my partner can do any dumb thing s/he wants and I can lose all of my personal assets to cover her/his mistakes?

A: Yes, that's right!

Scary, huh?

Legal partnerships

In legal partnerships, partners share in profits or losses in whatever proportion they have agreed to! Any profit or loss is reported on his or her own personal income tax return. Although there is no legal filing requirement for partnership agreements, you can see why they are highly advisable.

There are some things *partners cannot* legally do. Here are a few examples:

- A partner cannot secretly obtain for himself/herself an opportunity available to the partnership.

- Partnership assets cannot be diverted for personal use.

- Partners cannot fail to distribute partnership profits to other members.

There are certainly more, but this just gives you an idea of some common partnership "don'ts."

"Limited Partnerships" are a different animal, and there are legal requirements for them. These have a "General Partner" who really runs things, and "Limited Partners" who are basically investors. That means they fall under security laws.

LLCs have many of the benefits of partnerships and provide protection from the liability being passed on to put personal assets at risk – thus the name "*Limited Liability Company.*"

Get professional advice

The "Smart Thing to Know" is to engage the services of qualified professionals – attorneys and/or accountants – to help you structure any legal partnerships you form, especially those that might incur liabilities. Otherwise, you may (unknowingly) put your personal wealth/possessions at risk, and that is *not* a smart thing to do!

The Uniform Partnership Act was adopted widely in the US (in most, but not all states – check with your state) to define some of these rules of partnerships, and provide awareness and warnings to those entering legal partnerships. If your country has such a law, its provisions will likely cover any partnership you form – so check it out, and make sure you comply.

Oral agreements = misunderstandings

Oral partnership agreements are not advisable. It is too easy to have misunderstandings, which are simply impossible to resolve. Memo-

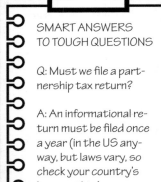

SMART ANSWERS
TO TOUGH QUESTIONS

Q: Must we file a partnership tax return?

A: An informational return must be filed once a year (in the US anyway, but laws vary, so check your country's laws on this.).

KILLER QUESTIONS

Shouldn't we do something to limit our personal liability?

ries are inaccurate, and become more so under pressure. Even minor disagreements can escalate into major arguments. Partners do not have to be "equal partners" in partnerships – in fact many times they are not. In professional partnerships (lawyers, doctors, etc.) all partners must be members of the profession. Partners in legal partnerships usually don't get salaries; they periodically take an agreed-upon share of the income from the business (this is often called a "draw").

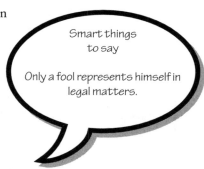

Smart things
to say

Only a fool represents himself in
legal matters.

Not every active joining of interests makes people partners, either for tax purposes or legally. Mere co-owners might not be partners provided that they don't actively carry on a business with whatever they own jointly. Sharing of expenses for a project doesn't necessarily make people "legal" partners either – but it might – so do your homework!

Finally, remember this point again – partners, as well as the partnership are liable for the legal obligations of the partnership – personally!

Upfront preparations

Now that I have incited you to action (I hope), I need to slow you down for just a moment. Have you really done your homework? Go back and read the prior sections about setting goals, etc. Do you realistically know what you want from this partnership, and what the prospective partner wants?

If you don't, think about it. And discuss it with people inside your organization. Then discuss it with your partner. Most partnerships fail because sticky issues were not discussed upfront. They then become buried landmines waiting to blow up the partnership at some crucial time.

Make sure you both understand each other's objectives. Verify the resource needs and timing. Discuss longer-term implications and where opportunities might arise or problems might occur. Conflicts are certain to arise. Discuss how to deal with them, and at what level, and specifically who will handle which kinds of conflicts. You don't need a big meeting to resolve every little thing that comes up – but you will need one when something big comes up.

SMART PEOPLE
TO HAVE ON
YOUR SIDE

> "When your objectives are not aligned, expect discord."
>
> Jordan Lewis

Communicate

As you discuss expectations, discuss measures and feedback and how everyone will stay "on board." Communications – make that good, honest, open communications – are the grease that makes the partnership machine work. Grease is used in machines to reduce friction. All machines have friction. So do all partnerships. Learn how, when and where to apply the grease – communications. Unlike grease, which is intended to be used sparingly, communications is best used liberally, but selectively.

SMART VOICES

"If it can't be measured, it can't be managed."

Will Kaydos, president,
The Decision Group

If you and your prospective partner have agreed on the goals and objectives, measures and feedback, then you must also agree on when, where and how communications will occur to keep the relationship working smoothly and minimizing unnecessary friction. Some friction – not too much – is fine, normal and even healthy. Too much heats things up and when things get heated up (like tempers) bad results usually follow.

```
PARTNERSHIP CHECKPOINTS

• Outcomes: What is success, specifics?
• Benefits: What's in it for me/us? ... (and what do we risk to get how much
  out of it?)
• Barriers: What problems might we face?
• Approach: How will this partnership work?
• Support: What support do I have or need to provide?
• Measurement: How will we measure results and reward shared success?

Source: Development Dimensions International, Partnerships: Creating
Synergy
```

Checkpoints for progress

Choosing the checkpoints for progress in partnerships and alliances is like choosing a custom-made suit – it varies from person to person, company to company. But just because it is widely variable, that is no excuse to skip a critical step. I have talked about issues like goals and objectives, trust and balanced risks and rewards *ad infinitum*.

What it comes down to is deciding honestly what you expect from the partnership or alliance. It also comes down to understanding what your partner expects. Then the challenge is to define the steps on the path to success in some finite ways so you can use these as milestones or checkpoints.

Is your goal market penetration of new markets? Then measure market shares, but don't forget to define what you think success would be upfront, so all partners can reach consensus on it. An old colleague, Dr Ramon Leon of the College of Business Administration, University of Tennessee, Knoxville taught me years ago – "Define success so you will recognize it when you have achieved it." Then he advised that you raise your sights in the next

MEASURING PARTNERSHIPS

Since both parties must benefit from the partnership, both parties must have identified and quantified some expected benefits. These should be the top-level indicators of the partnership's success.

Some examples of measurable benefits might be lower costs, faster response to market, shorter order cycle time, shorter product development time, reduced inventories, better quality, lower costs.

Ask yourself questions like these:

- Are your partners doing better for you than the industry norms?
- How does their rate of improving costs, productivity, and quality compare with others?
- What services, products, information, etc. are exchanged between the partners?
- Is one partner responding or performing better than the other with respect to making the partnership work?

Quality of products and services in a supplier-user relationship should obviously be measured. This includes incoming product quality and product/service problems discovered further down the line. Quality should especially be measured at the interface(s) of the partners to verify they are both meeting their obligations. Neither alone is responsible for quality – they both are. Processes critical to the partnership must also be measured to assure they are working as they should.

- Are specifications correct? Frequently revised? Well communicated?
- Are orders placed on time? Delivery schedules changed? Lead-time needs considered?
- How do partners respond to each other's needs? In good times and in bad times?

Partnership activities should also be measured to assure the things that are supposed to happen, do happen. Activities do not assure results, but it's impossible to get results without them. How many meetings between appropriate managers? How frequently are meetings held?

- How many benchmarking/comparison activities have been performed with partners?
- How many front-line employees visit partners each year? Are these "home and home" (2-way) visits?
- How much help has been provided to partners to understand your business, improve their operations, and improve communications – and vice-versa?
- Where have they helped you? Where have you helped them?
- What improvements to processes on both sides have been made as a result of the partnership?

What measurable improvement in the performance of each partner's business is evident as a result of this partnership – better customer service, greater market penetration, improved quality, higher productivity, increased profit margin, and so forth.

In other words, is it affecting the top line in revenue and the bottom line in profit and return on assets? If it isn't, it probably isn't working!

Always remember, "If you don't measure it, you can't understand it, control it, or improve it."

Will Kaydos, president, The Decision Group and author of *Measuring, Managing, and Maximizing Performance*, Productivity Press, 1991, and *Operational Performance Measurement*, St Lucie Press, 1999

step, but not overlook the importance of defining what would be considered a successful outcome.

Too often, people are fuzzy about what success really is. Then when the time comes to agree on whether the partnership has been successful, they become guilty of convenient memory lapses. This is devastating to people and partnerships. It is hard enough to measure and set checkpoints without creating unfulfilled expectations or failing to recognize real success when it is achieved.

Smart quotes

"Too often we're sending bad data or best-guess data to our trading partners and optimizing around that ... We end up with longer lead times and bigger inventory levels because we don't have confidence in the system."

Beth Enslow, VP, Descartes Systems Group, from "The Glass Pipeline," *Supply Chain Management Software Supplement*, Cahners, 2000

Obstacles and pitfalls

Misunderstandings will lead the list. Here are some comments you will hear when misunderstandings occur.

- "I heard that, but you say you said this."

- "I heard you say that, but I didn't know you meant 'all the time.'"

- " Nobody mentioned that when we were planning this."

- "We just don't have the _____ (people, money, time, resources – pick one or more) to do that. I can't imagine who promised we would or could do it."

- "Did you hear what they did?"

- "Who said that?"

- "Don't blame me, I didn't do (or say, or promise) that."

These phrases and many more like them will burn in your ears. You've probably heard them before. Misunderstandings lead to obstacles and pitfalls on the best of partnership journeys. The only way to avoid them is ... (you guessed it) ... communicate upfront!

When partnerships get started on the right foot, and understanding is good, wonderful things can happen. Here is an example of one that got started right.

A PARTNERSHIP SUCCESS STORY

When I write about things based on what has happened around me there is at least a reasonable comfort that they are (or were) true. Even this is based on my own perspective. In their more lucid moments most managers and executives realize they receive mostly managed information from the organization designed to make them feel good. This "filtered input" has always concerned me. That concern keeps me constantly on the lookout for cases that either reinforce (or contradict) my beliefs. That is where this story came from.

It was a sunny spring day in Knoxville (TN, USA) when I arrived at the modern APS offices within a stone's throw of Interstate 75 and 40. (If you've been through Knoxville on those highways, the office is right about where the traffic jams usually occur.) The president of APS and the HR manager greeted me. Then the fun began.

They described how APS is a partner with Navistar (the industrial truck maker) and does much of Navistar's basic accounting work. As I asked questions and they described how they worked, their vocabulary and signals all

---

pointed to this being the kind of powerful partnership which makes "outsourcing" no longer a dirty word. Companies can only afford to invest in and develop the things that are part of their core competencies. For many companies, keeping the books, and paying or collecting the bills has precious little to do with those competencies.

At APS, this is what they do best. Navistar wanted this kind of service and after selecting three smaller cities where they felt costs might be lower; they found Knoxville and APS. APS is a company created specifically to serve Navistar. They started with around 50 people (please don't call them "temps" because they really aren't).

Navistar sets the "boundaries" of what authority they have. APS formed teams – self-directed teams – to work within those boundaries. The teams are organized around the kind of work to be done. One team keeps the general ledger. Another pays suppliers. A third pays other bills including travel costs. A series of teams are split by the type of customer, and take care of invoicing. The last team is a general support team.

The offices are physically organized so the teams are together in close proximity. The camaraderie is evident. Some team members are cross-trained to move between jobs and even between teams. There are over 80 people now, and there is no doubt among them who their customer – and partner – is. It is Navistar. There are Navistar employees on site, but the number is down from twelve at the start to just eight now. The savings to Navistar are millions of dollars per year, directly due to this partnership.

The most successful partnerships are based on choosing good partners to start with. There must be something of comparable value for both partners in the partnership. That is the case here. Open sharing of information is critical. The immediate answer to my question of whether Navistar knew how much profit APS makes was "of course they do." When I asked about the future, they cited two simple goals: Stay abreast of Navistar's needs, and find another partner/company to create another success for APS. Their answer about competition was even refreshing. "We don't focus on competition. We're busy taking care of our customer." I would describe this as a model partnership.

They get a lot of visitors (like me) to see how they are doing it. The physical surroundings don't tell the story. The attitudes, behavior and values of the people make the difference. That is a little harder to "see," but it's there if you look closely. Small groups of two or three people discussing business in their adjacent cubicles or over the short (4½ ft.) partitions that separate the team members. Eight people doing some "group learning" in front of a TV monitor, easel and podium in the lunchroom. A busy, but not frantic work pace in a quiet, but "doing the job" atmosphere. Smiles greet the visitors and management. A sidebar conversation occupies the president briefly here and there.

Surprisingly, not all the information came in electronically. There was still a lot of paper shuffling. That just represents another opportunity. I believe they'll capitalize on it. When they have really arrived, some of their contacts at Navistar that aren't familiar with them will even stop referring to them as the "temp agency." They will be happier when that happens.

How long can such a partnership last? As long as the people involved choose to keep it together. Changing the people changes the dynamics of the relationship, and that can either strengthen or tear apart partnerships. The choice is that of the partners.

Meanwhile, the future of the business world holds much uncertainty. Rapid, unpredictable change is one of the few things on which most people can agree. Being good at too many things is neither practicable nor profitable. The successful companies of the future will be able to react to change with incredible speed and flexibility by shifting their shape to create and deliver value better than their competitors – by being very good at what they *do* – and doing just what they are very good at.

The cornerstones of such a rapid "shape-shift" are partnerships with highly competent, closely linked partners. On that sunny spring afternoon, I was able to see a partnership success story right there next to I-75 and 40. The interstate traffic was starting to back up at 4 p.m. but things were moving smoothly at the Navistar/APS partnership. My beliefs were reinforced. It was a good day.

Successes and failures

Culture mismatches usually fail as partnerships. Somehow the people just think differently and have different beliefs and values and ways of doing things. More often than not, these differences give rise to arguments and disagreements in which neither party can quite understand how the other could hold such a position. Consider the example below and you'll see what I mean – even when the partnership is an acquisition.

TOYSMART.COM AND DISNEY = A CLASH OF CULTURES

The failure of toysmart.com and its alliance with Disney is a classic case of the parent (Disney) and the upstart (toysmart.com) having big differences in culture-based strategy – in perceptions and measures of success and the path to achieve it. Toysmart.com was a startup and an innovator, but without much structure or discipline, waiting for consumers to guide its marketing tactics. Disney is an old line, deliberative giant, which was (appropriately) concerned about the intersection of this new startup with its existing cash-cow businesses and valuable brand franchises.

While toysmart.com argued about the wisdom of Disney forcing them to advertise on Disney media to conserve cash, and whether that limitation was critical to their success or failure, competitors were moving on. What is certain is that toysmart.com's strategy and tactics were not sufficiently well formed and agreed upon at the influential levels of both companies – but especially Disney.

As toysmart.com under-delivered on expectations, it kept adjusting and spending to gain customers. Disney deliberated more and delayed decisions. Who was right? It is hard to say without knowing all of the facts and circumstances at the time these decisions were being made (or not made). Ultimately, the upstart perished. Was it Disney's fault? Was it toysmart.com's fault? Who knows? Probably some parts of both companies were at fault. Culture clashes make for messy partnerships, and usually fail.

The result was, of course, disaster. The lesson: Don't ignore widely differing cultures. Take the time to figure out what you plan to do, and approximately how. *Get all of the important decision-makers on board and then act fast.*

What can go wrong – and what to do when it does

When a partnership starts to flounder and fail, rapid decisive action is needed. Here are a couple of basic steps to take that can remedy a sick partnership.

Get all of the partnership originators together and start by reviewing why this partnership was formed in the first place – to collaborate on something together – and to get something out of it.

Then check the assumptions made upfront. Has something changed? What? Is it a "show-stopper?" Be sure you are dealing with all levels of the organization(s). Lower levels can't make policy to overcome problems and may be having or causing trouble because of that.

Higher levels can make policy but usually don't have a clue as to the real issues and details that might be causing problems at the levels where the real work gets done. Make sure that the understanding is clear, before policy makers jump in. Remember that these are usually Type A "fixers" and because that is how they got to the top, they may be inclined to act first, ask questions later. That is bad voodoo for a partnership. (I know, I've been there, and done that!) Remember a good partnership is a top-to-bottom, across-the-organization relationship.

SMART VOICES	"Starting an alliance without having a clear understanding of the cultural dynamics and organizational forces resistant to change is like playing Russian roulette." Source: Booz·Allen and Hamilton, *A Practical Guide to Alliances: Leapfrogging the Learning Curve*, 1993

A sad story – of what could and did go wrong!

The dot-coms death throes have torpedoed many of the partnerships and alliances that flourished and got so much press coverage in the growth days, before reality set in. Here is just one example – but there are hundreds of these out there. Again, coincidentally, toysmart.com and Disney are involved.

KELLOGG BITES IT WITH TOYSMART.COM

"... many of the once-hot co-marketing partnerships have become embarrassing fiascos that executives hesitate to discuss ... Just ask cereal giant Kellogg. Last spring [2000], the Battle Creek, Michigan [US] company forged a co-marketing deal with toysmart.com. Boxes of Froot Loops® and Frosted Flakes® were co-branded with an online loyalty program called 'Eet and Ern'. But in May, just three weeks after the boxes arrived on store shelves, toysmart.com's backer, Disney, pulled the plug on the toy retailer ... Kellogg says its ill-fated alliance with toysmart.com had no negative impact on its time-tested cereal brands. After all, the boxes weren't on the shelves long enough for consumers to fully associate Kellogg with toysmart.com." What else could Kellogg say? Or do? If the promotion was a good partnership idea when they did it, when did it turn into a bad one? When the partner "went south" and went out of business. Now that is a serious obstacle to a partnership!

Bad partnerships happen all the time

The dot-com collapse is not the sole or even the major cause of partnerships gone wrong. There are many causes, ranging from poor choices of partners, to poor planning of the partnership combination, to poisoning the partnership with power wielded by one of the partners. A few of these have become landmarks of pitiful partnering.

Smart quotes

"Murphy's Law: If something can go wrong, it will, and at the worst possible time."

Union Pacific and Southern Pacific Railroads looked like the ideal partners. The combination would create a seamless network of rail service from the Midwestern US to the West Coast. And it did – except for one small problem. The actual execution of the partnership combination was botched so badly that the result was rail gridlock in some areas, lost trains in others, and a near national scale calamity in the US. The railroads cut too many people, did not manage the information systems combination properly and lost control of the sprawling rail network and the trains traveling on it.

HFS and CUC was a $14 billion (US) partnership to create Cendant which was supposed to be a marketing powerhouse. Well, not exactly. Someone allegedly "cooked the books" – a term that described accounting irregularities that caused a federal investigation and hammered the stock price. Insurer Conseco's acquisition of lender Green Tree Financial was supposed to be a "slam dunk" too – until Green Tree was hit with huge charges for bad loans. Maybe they got their loan advice from the Japanese, whose banks seem to have a lock on bad loan problems for the past few years.

"There are two kinds of 'no-brainers' in business, those situations that are so easy 'no brains' are needed, and those that are misunderstood or underestimated and 'no brains' are used! The former is no problem. The latter is a big problem!"

Smart things to say about partnerships

Smart things
to say

"Some partnerships remind me
of a ham and egg breakfast. The
chicken makes a meaningful con-
tribution, but the pig is the
one who is totally com-
mitted!"

Finally, in a saga that is still unfolding, there is the so-called "merger of equals" myth that Daimler-Benz perpetrated on Chrysler. It was actually an acquisition, but nobody told Chrysler until it was a "done deal." Now, with the "brain trust" that built Chrysler either leaving or being driven out by the German leadership, the entire company is foundering. Chrysler's people are demoralized at best, and devastated at worst. Mercedes-Benz is still making good money, but most of it is going to cover Chrysler's losses. Maybe it is getting what it deserves. *What goes around, comes around,* is the old saying.

To top off this mismanaged partnership, DaimlerChrysler is now mandating that its suppliers (they used to be called partners) give them five percent price discounts immediately, and an additional ten percent over the next two years. These are the same suppliers who were Chrysler's partners in helping save millions of dollars and increase Chrysler's speed and innovation so greatly over the past decade. It appears that DaimlerChrysler's new management interpretation of a good partnership *is "they give and we take."*

Already several large suppliers have called back deliveries – unheard of in the auto industry. But 65 percent of Chrysler's content comes from suppliers, and pushing them around may turn out to be the dumbest decision of the decade for DaimlerChrysler. "If they think we're still going to be bringing them our best technology, they're crazy," is how one angry supplier puts it. Clearly this is a formerly successful partnership that is coming unglued.

PARTNERSHIP ADVICE

Do

- Take the initiative. Talk to people. Think creatively about ways to work with others to achieve common goals.
- Put ideas down in writing when you believe people are interested. Make sure to represent these as ideas rather than as an agreement.
- Clearly define the objectives of a potential partnership, the resources that each participant would bring to the activity, and the benefits that each stands to gain.
- Be inclusive. Early on, involve people whose approval or participation will ultimately be required.
- Learn about prospective partners; assess your comfort level with their reputation and capabilities before joining the partnership.
- Be realistic in estimating the often-lengthy time periods required to initiate and implement a partnership.
- Investigate alternative strategies for achieving your objective. Are other avenues or other partners better suited to accomplish the objectives?

Don't

- Limit yourself in the ways you use partnerships to further company objectives.
- Wait until the last minute to bring in supervisors, public affairs, or general counsel to review the contemplated partnership.
- Get into personal battles.

Source: *IndustryWeek*, April 3, 1995, excerpted from *Environmental Partnerships: A Business Handbook* by the Management Institute of Environment and Business, Harcourt Brace, 1995

7
Partnership is Collaboration

THE POWER OF PEOPLE WORKING TOGETHER
TO SUCCEED

THE SIX SMARTEST THINGS TO KNOW ABOUT PARTNERSHIPS

No one is good enough to succeed alone.
Whoever chooses the best partners, wins!
Trust is a must – and a two-way street.
There has to be enough in it for both partners.
No support from the top means "no deal."
Power is poison to partnerships.

As you read this chapter, you may say "why so much emphasis on collaboration?" The answer is that all partnerships are, in varying degrees, some kind of collaborative effort. There must be other fundamentals: well thought out strategy, attention to execution, plenty of communication, and of course, trust. But, some partnerships are lousy ones, and some are great ones, and most fall somewhere in the middle. That is why learning about how to collaborate effectively will make you "smart" about building better partnerships.

Succeeding together is fun and depends on people

SMART VOICES

"It's easy to get good players. Getting 'em to play together effectively, that's the hard part."

Casey Stengel, manager, New York Yankees

Did you ever notice that society places a premium on people who get things done? They usually get paid more, get promoted more often and generally seem to be better liked and they are also more energized by their work and life overall. People who get things done are often the most active volunteer leaders in church and community organizations too. Why?

Because they seem to know *how* to get things done! Mind you, these people don't do it all themselves – they find partners who help them. They may do very little of what it is that needs to get done. What they do very well is to get other people to cooperate with them and help them get things done. What they do even better is to get people to collaborate with them.

Cooperation is kind of a passive, "I'll go along with you and help with that" attitude. Collaboration is a more active, "Let me help you with that, because I know another, better way to do it" mindset. When you set out to do something, you're limited by your own knowledge and abilities (and physical resources too!). When a group sets out to do the same thing and they partner to cooperate with each other, the task usually gets done faster and more easily. When that group decides to really put their minds together and collaborate on getting the job done, it gets done more effectively, too.

Smart quotes

"We long to participate in a meaningful workplace where we are appreciated for our contributions."

Stephen M. Dent

The best way to capitalize on opportunities is by using the collective knowledge of a group of people collaborating. You may mistakenly think you have to operate alone. You don't – in fact, far from it. You may think that passive or active cooperation is enough, but it isn't – if you want the best outcome. Collaborating means that you bring your knowledge and contribute this knowledge openly and freely. In partnering efforts, teamwork and collaboration often get confused.

Smart quotes

"Participative management is not democratic. Having a say differs from having a vote."

Max DePree

Abraham Maslow is still right. Douglas McGregor was too. Who are these two guys? They are two men who studied why people behave in certain ways. What they found was that people behave in certain ways because of feelings, beliefs and values they have developed in their lives and situations in which they live and work. The motivation of people is the topic of hundreds of books, but the work of these two people is important because it helps explain why people behave the way they do – in business, in life, and in collaborative partnerships. To succeed in collaboration, partnerships and with people working together, it is important to understand what motivates people to behave the way they do.

Douglas McGregor attempted to categorize the motivation of people into two, rather simplistic, but actually quite profound types. He called them Theory X and Theory Y. There has since been a Theory Z developed, but that one comes closer to self-motivation and relates more to Maslow's works. If you want more information on McGregor's theories, you can read his great classic book titled *Human Side of Enterprise* (McGraw Hill 1985 reprint). Here are his basic theories:

Smart quotes

"Partnerships may be a necessity, but teamwork is tough. And that's a lesson that many are about to find out the hard way."

James Daly

Theory X

"The average human being has an inherent dislike of work and will avoid it if he can ... and prefers to be directed, wishes to avoid responsibility, has little ambition and wants security above all. Most people must be coerced, directed and threatened with punishment ... "

Theory Y

" ... physical and mental effort in work is as natural as play or rest ... External control and threat of punishment are not the only means for bringing about effort toward organizational objectives. The average human being learns, under proper conditions not only to accept but to seek responsibility."

Maslow's brilliant original book on human motivation had such an unusual title (*Eupsychian Management*) that it attracted little attention. Fortunately, it has now been reissued with additional commentary under the title *Maslow on Management* (Wiley 1998). The centerpiece of Maslow's principles was a pyramid-shaped hierarchy of needs, which motivate human behavior. If you remember these, you will understand why people involved in collaboration or partnerships behave the way they do (see Fig. 7.1).

Smart quotes

"The musician must make music, an artist must paint, a poet must write, if he is to ultimately be at peace with himself. What a man can be, he must be."

Abraham Maslow

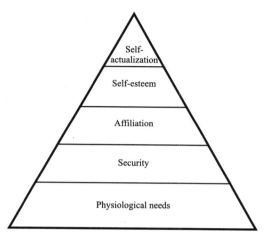

Fig. 7.1 Maslow's Hierarchy of Needs

What is collaboration?

All partnerships depend on collaboration between people – between members of both partner organizations. Many people would say such collaboration is teamwork, and that is close, but not quite right. Teamwork has become an over-worked word in the past two decades. Teamwork is not always collaboration – although collaboration is usually good teamwork. Let's start with a definition of collaboration.

Collaboration is an act of shared creation or shared discovery. At the heart of collaboration is the desire to create something, discover something, solve some sort of problem, or get something done.

That should be the case with team efforts, but it isn't always. Too often, teams are formed by just assembling a group of people. They are assigned a purpose that is sometimes unclear, and given a set of goals (if any are defined at all) that they had nothing to do with choosing. These people are a long way from a

"The Partnership Continuum Model ... is the blueprint for creating successful partnerships. This model has been used successfully by thousands of people."

Stephen M. Dent

shared creation or discovery. Maybe a problem-solving effort is the team's assigned purpose. Even then they are supposed to figure out how to be good team members while they figure out how to solve the problem. The two challenges are not even related – the first involves interpersonal and group interaction, and the second requires problem identification and problem-solving skills.

One part of collaboration is a relationship

Throwing together a group of people no more ensures a relationship or makes them a team than dumping a bunch of ingredients in a bowl ensures that a cake will result. Unfortunately, this is an all-too-common solution of time-starved management. "Form a team and assign it a clearly defined set

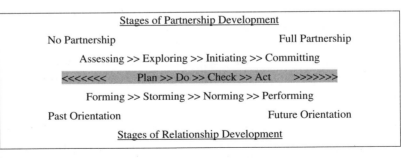

Stages of Partnership Development

No Partnership   Full Partnership

Assessing >> Exploring >> Initiating >> Committing

<<<<<<<   Plan >> Do >> Check >> Act   >>>>>>>

Forming >> Storming >> Norming >> Performing

Past Orientation   Future Orientation

Stages of Relationship Development

Fig. 7.2 The Partnership Continuum Model. Source: Stephen M. Dent, *Partnering Intelligence*, Davies-Black 1999, reprinted with permission

Smart quotes

"Organizations that attempt to substitute increased communication for increased collaboration will learn the hard way that there is a tremendous difference."

Michael Schrage

of goals and objectives" turns into "draft a bunch of unsuspecting people, and call them a team" and then tell them to figure out how to solve this nagging problem and hope they do.

Don't confine your definition of collaboration to a single group or team of people. That is not how it works in many cases. The most powerful partnership collaborations are spontaneous ones, which may involve several groups. The people involved work together in a technical sense, but not necessarily in a literal sense. When a loose-knit group of people from different areas, departments or companies decide to partner and really collaborate, tremendous breakthroughs can happen.

Teamwork as part of a single team can become monotonous, because similar problems often require similar solutions and the team members will fall into familiar, comfortable roles. You do this; I do that; someone else does something else. This is not collaboration – it is simply a division of work. This may have been collaboration the first time we went through it, but it is not any more. Collaboration is original. Circumstances are constantly changing. Thus the team described above is not really collaborating – it is just going through the motions.

Another part of collaboration is a process

Let's consider a more complete definition of collaboration: *Collaboration is the process of two or more people with complementary skills and/or knowledge interacting to create a shared understanding where none had existed, using understanding to create something, discover something, solve some problem, or get something done.*

Nothing in that definition says these people need to be part of a team – or a partnership! They may not even need to be in the same place at the same time. What is important is that they engage in a process – a series of steps in a defined order that will lead to a desired outcome.

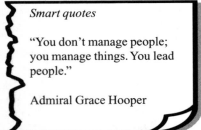

Smart quotes

"You don't manage people; you manage things. You lead people."

Admiral Grace Hooper

All collaboration is not just touchy-feely stuff either. Sometimes the collaboration that leads partnerships to work must be hard-nosed, requires strong leadership, and results in conflicts over disagreements. These conflicts require resolution, which is not always easy (in fact, it is usually hard!). Even with these "hard" sounding words to describe the series of events in the process, collaboration can work, and lead to powerful partnerships – but only if the people who are the partners want it to work.

Collaboration is the end of a series of steps

A group must go through a series of steps on the way to collaboration. Partners are not immune from following these same group interaction steps. Sociologists have a shorthand set of terms, which describe this sequence (you'll see these same terms in Stephen Dent's Partnership Continuum diagram with other elements surrounding them):

- *forming* (getting to know each other);

- *storming* (fighting for control, power, etc.);

- *norming* (arriving at accepted group norms for how things are done and people behave); and

- *performing* (Getting on with the successful work).

Other sets of collaborative teamwork steps are shown in Fig. 7.2 (p. 162) and in Table 7.1 below. It would be nice to jump right to cooperation or collaboration, but unfortunately, it is often hard to skip the earlier steps. Note the tough terms used to describe the steps. This is no cakewalk!

Table 7.1 Relationship stages of collaborative teamwork

Peer Relations	Stance	Key Characteristics
Combative	fighting	Aggression, resistance, damage
Competitive	striving	Rivalry, mixed motivations
Cooperative	agreeing	Acquiescence, obedience
Collaborative	partnering	Synergistic, interactive

Source: Tom Morris, *If Aristotle Ran General Motors*, Henry Holt and Company, New York, 1997

The best you can hope for is to move past the most difficult steps quickly and positively. The important thing is to know about all these steps, and to avoid poisoning the relationships in their early stages. It will be much harder to get to collaboration if the storming or combative stage becomes bitter and hurtful.

SMART VOICES

A partnership is like a team. When a key player in the process changes, the whole chemistry changes and the team must go through the whole teaming process of forming, storming and norming again. It can create quite a bit of dysfunction for a while, if not handled properly.

Bill Lake, president, Royal Medica USA

Constructive disagreement

There is a widespread misunderstanding that to be a good team member and a positive collaborator means to agree with the group or be quiet when you disagree or don't understand. Nothing could be further from the truth. Powerful collaborative efforts come from constructive disagreement. Good partners, like good team members, must be honest with each other. (Remember CHIPs.)

Constructive disagreement is flexible, always trying to see other viewpoints that might change a person's perspective and position. Destructive disagreement is a "take it or leave it" mentality, one which says, in effect, "I'm right, you're wrong, end of discussion!" Failure to understand, denies you the ability to be a collaborator. The only dumb question is the one that is not asked. Understanding allows everyone involved to pool knowledge and viewpoints. Even if you have no new knowledge to apply to the solution, sometimes just a different viewpoint will expose new solutions.

FOUR POWERFUL STATEMENTS TO BUILD PARTNERSHIP RELATIONS

- "Will you help me, please?"
- "I'm sorry, I don't understand."
- "I don't know, but I will find out and get back to you" – and then be sure to do it.
- The hardest: "I'm sorry, I was wrong."

Understanding the task is one of the most important ingredients in collaboration – what problem must be solved or what new discovery or creation is desired. Another important part of collaboration is saying what you will do – and then doing what you said you would – because others are depending on you to hold up your end of the deal.

Collaborating in a crisis can happen faster than collaborating simply to generate positive change. Crisis collaboration is also easier to get started, but harder to sustain, especially after the immediate crisis is resolved. Many companies partner and pull together when their existence is threatened, only to see the partnership fall apart after they have weathered the storm. For real collaboration to occur, trust must exist. Talking about collaborative behavior is "easy," but achieving true collaboration is "hard work."

PARTNERSHIPS THAT WORKED – FOR A WHILE – HUFFY'S GOOD NEWS, BAD NEWS STORY

The year was 1984. The US bicycle market was under attack by the Taiwanese. Prices at retail and wholesale levels were dropping more than one percent every month. Imported bikes, which had reached a low point in 1982 at 16 percent of the US market, would blow past the 25 percent level, headed for a high of 57 percent in 1987. New Taiwanese bike "makers" were springing up like weeds after a spring rain. The number would reach over 100 before the battle reached its peak. This was nothing new for the US bike manufacturers. About every 10 to 15 years another country would come after this large, lucrative ($1 billion plus), and open market. It was Europe in the 1950s and 1960s, then Japan in the 1970s, and now Taiwan, with Korea warming up to be next, and the monster of China lurking in the shadows just over the horizon.

In the late 1970s, US manufacturers had been clamoring to add capacity to supply the continually rising demand. The market had doubled in size every decade for the past 40 years and peaked with the US discovery of the ten-speed racer in the early 1970s. This uncomfortable, relatively fragile machine imported from Europe caught the fancy of US gas-starved, recreation- and fitness-focused population and drove the US market past the 14 million bike peak in 1973, only to crash to just half that level by 1975. In 1982–83, the recession in the United States, combined with the advent of video games, siphoned away purchasing dollars and caused the US bike market to bottom at under 7 million units annually. This was down from the 1979 peak of 11 million.

The US bike manufacturers not wiped out by that double-dip collapse were likely to fall to the attack of the Taiwanese with a labor force paid less than $1.00/hour and a burgeoning bicycle component industry migrating there from Japan (where autos and electronics were becoming king).

In the early 1980s, ten-speed bikes were selling at retail prices of $89–99, with an occasional promotion at $79. Kids' 16" and 20" (wheel) bikes were often priced at $59–69 and seldom promoted below $50. Then came the Taiwan imports, sporting features, styling and paint jobs that had been yielding $10–20 or more in retail premiums, and selling at prices that let discounters like Target sell imported ten-speeds at $69 with better margins than domestic supplied products at $79! Just as the US manufacturers figured out how to squeeze down their costs and margins to compete at this level, retail prices dropped again – to $59 for ten speeds and $49 for kids' bikes! The US dollar strengthened until it traded for 40 of the NT$, and aggressive importers were having a field day.

It was this intimidating scenario that faced Huffy Bicycles in 1984. Huffy held 22 percent of the US bike market – all produced in Celina, OH (US). Imports were still below 20 percent. In 1987, Huffy still held 22 percent; imports were at 57 percent. By 1991, imports were sliding below the 45 percent mark, the US dollar was worth only 25 NT$, and Huffy was up to 33 percent share (limited only by its capacity to produce). The bottom of the price slide had seen wholesale prices drop over 25 percent. Huffy had maintained its share and profitability by reducing costs almost the same amount. The question was, how?

The answer is not as simple as a single word, but one word sums up the pivotal element of it: *Partnerships*! Huffy Bicycles had formed a cooperative "partnership" with its 2000 employees, and with its United Steel Workers union. It formed partnerships with (a reduced number of) the best suppliers both in the US and abroad. It formed partnerships with a select group of leading retailers like Wal*Mart, Toys "R" Us, Kmart, Target, Price Club, and Sears and many others. Huffy had also formed partnerships with a small, select group of outside resources to help shape its strategic thrust, including its sales rep firms, consultants Ram Charan, Roger Blackwell, Andersen Consulting, and Mitchell Fein (the founder of Improshare), Lois USA, its advertising agency, and the local government and educational institutions.

These partnerships alone would not have been sufficient if it were it not for a lot of hard work, innovation, cooperation, and more than a little luck. But one thing is certain: without these partners, their support, and the combined power of partners pulling together, the history of Huffy Bicycles, and in fact, Huffy Corporation, would be very different indeed.

Adapted from: John L. Mariotti, *The Power of Partnerships*, Blackwell, 1995

**PostScript*: In the next decade, the pressure of Chinese bicycle competition proved to be too much for Huffy and its US competitors/counterparts to withstand. At this writing, all US bicycle manufacturing plants of Huffy and its primary US competitors have been closed, and the products are now all imported from China. The market has climbed to record levels of unit volume, and 16" and 20" (wheel) children's bikes are now retailing for as low as $29 – and all of the profit has been wrung out of them – for everyone in the supply chain! Many of Huffy's partners survived, but many more are gone; a few are still the leading US retailers, and Asian bike component manufacturers, but the 2000 Huffy employees no longer work in a Huffy plant. Even the strongest partnerships cannot overcome immense differences in labor costs when design and production technology can be easily transferred around the globe in a short time.

THE IMPEDIMENTS TO COLLABORATION

- Doing things the old way (natural resistance to change).
- Conventional accounting practices (traditional vs. cross-company).
- Tax laws ("price paid" and "price sold" obscure indirect costs).
- Limited viewpoint (silo organizations, functional fixations).
- Annual negotiations (adversarial, waste time and energy).
- Time investment (it takes time and hard work).
- Inadequate communication (a big issue).
- Inconsistent behavior (disrupts trust).
- Betrayal (destroys trust and everything else!).

Derived from: John T. Mentzer, James H. Foggin, and Susan L. Golicic, "Collaboration – The Enablers, Impediments, and Benefits" *Supply Chain Management Review*, September–October, 2000

Smart quotes

"All our dreams can come true – if we have the courage to pursue them."

Walt Disney

Working together with a partner is more fun

To get things done through collaboration partners work together toward a common, agreed-upon set of goals. Until the goals are agreed upon, there is a danger that the collaboration will be fragmented and not cohesive. This wastes energy and demoralizes people, which in turn can jeopardize a partnership effort.

A group that wants to get something done must encourage collaboration by valuing the input of its members – even when that input does not appear to be immediately useful. Managers, leaders and other people with authority can have one of two effects on collaboration – a stimulating one or a chilling one.

The stimulation comes from cases when the person in a lead or authority position genuinely appreciates the input and attempts to use it – or at least incorporate it into the thought processes as the group moves toward decisions. The chilling effect occurs when the person (or partner) in authority acts with disdain, disinterest or open contempt of the ideas presented. This is demeaning to the individual giving the ideas and chilling to the partnership's collaborative efforts.

Smart quotes

"Leadership: the art of getting someone else to do something you want done because he wants to do it."

Dwight Eisenhower (General and US President)

Smart people will try to use all the collaborative help they can get. Smart workers will recognize the kind of manager they have and conduct themselves accordingly – this means active collaboration with a good manager, and cautious input with a poor one. In either case, it is important to avoid becoming discouraged – even by a poor manager; they sometimes wake up and see the light as information accumulates and collaboration begins.

We are no longer in an age of bosses who can succeed by controlling and directing people. We are in an age of more and more partnerships. Things are changing so fast that people want and need influence over their own destiny. This means the opportunity for collaboration is great, but the leaders must change from old command and control behavior to the new one of leadership, motivation and involvement. Partners can do wonderful things together but, as an old friend used to say, "UGOTTAWANNA!"

The traditional way to control organizations was to have policies and procedures, which were followed and rigidly enforced. When conditions, circumstances and competition change rapidly, these old, rigid rules fail. They become inflexible, slow, obsolete, and ineffective. This is when collaborative groups of people can step forward to save the day. Misguided rules and poor policies can inhibit the formation and success of partnerships, too. Trust and CHIPs will beat policy manuals every time for assuring

Smart quotes

"Never tell people how to do things. Tell them what to do and they will surprise you with their ingenuity."

George Patton

that the right things get done the right way. Partnering and collaboration will help to assure that the right things are getting done.

Unfortunately, unless there is open information sharing across all of the so-called "boundaries" – between people, between departments, between offices or plants, and between customer and supplier companies, true collaboration is difficult or impossible. Without sharing of information, the collective knowledge of the groups involved is not used to solve the problems.

Smart quotes

"Build for your team a feeling of oneness, of dependence upon one another and of strength derived by unity."

Vince Lombardi (football coach)

To help with the formation of collaborative partnerships, a checklist follows this section. Read it. Heed it. Use it. Enjoy the outcome!

A CHECKLIST FOR SUCCESSFUL PARTNERSHIP COLLABORATION

- Form a group that is likely to cooperate first, then collaborate.
- There should be something in it for each member.
- Make sure the current situation is clearly understood by all constituencies.
- Establish the leadership and sponsorship of this collaborative group and identify the natural leaders.
- Set group goals and objectives, and discuss potential outcomes, time-tables, and resource needs.
- Establish measures of progress, both tangible and intangible and measure results and review how the group is getting them.
- Provide regular feedback and document progress and agreements. Keep records of disputed issues and communicate openly and often.
- Identify known obstacles and challenges and seek help in eliminating them.
- Build partnership relationships to gain help and sustain progress, but choose partners carefully.
- Concentrate on new learning through the collaboration. Apply collective wisdom of the group to test the outcomes.
- Celebrate and share the knowledge gained about collaborative success. Leave a legacy of successful collaborators to seed new teams.

Trust is essential to collaboration – without it, nothing good gets done.

Who collaborates?

Anybody can collaborate with someone else, but it is not always natural or easy. In some highly individualistic cultures it is not the natural tendency either. If one Korean competes with one Japanese, the Korean will usually win. If a team of Koreans competes with a team of Japanese, the Japanese will almost always win. Why? Because the Korean culture is more individualistic, and the Japanese culture is more collaborative.

"True collaboration is something that completely reengineers the relationship or transaction between trading partners ... "

Andrew White, vice-president of product strategy, Logility, quoted in *BusinessWeek*, March 26, 2001

SMART VOICES

If you are an American, your tendency is for you to rely only on yourself – not on others! Americans often pride themselves on being rugged individualists. But, collaboration is all about people trusting each other and working together to utilize combined knowledge to achieve goals that are shared, which couldn't be achieved alone.

One of the characteristics that made America successful during the past century was its ability to become a "melting pot" of cultures that could and did work together. Collaboration requires many different kinds of sharing – information, ideas, experience, aspirations, goals, responsibilities and, often, credit when it works, and blame when it doesn't.

Smart quotes

"There is no use whatsoever trying to help people who do not help themselves. You cannot push anyone up a ladder unless he is willing to climb himself.

Andrew Carnegie

Smart quotes

"You never achieve real success unless you like what you are doing."

Dale Carnegie (author)

Collaboration is difficult enough within the same company (intra-company), but even more challenging when it is between two independent companies (inter-company).

But wait a minute! What makes the "other guys" want to collaborate with you? This has to be the same motivation as any kind of partnering. There has to be something in it for them and the risk/reward balance has to be fair and equitable – not equal – just fair and acceptable to both parties. Collaboration is an intellectual give and take. If you take more than you give, others may decide to quit giving. If you give more than you take, others may decide to try harder to do their share of giving. It's sort of like the Golden Rule in practice: "Do unto others as you would have them do unto you!" What have I got to offer in exchange for your collaboration? How about satisfaction, a sense of belonging and contributing, a feeling of having created or discovered something new and important?

Partnerships require change – beware of resistance to change

Smart things to say

The only one who likes change is a wet baby.

Change is frightening to everyone at some level – the more you have to risk, the more resistant to change you usually are. Resistance to change takes many forms, but a few of them are familiar. If you recognize them, you can begin to deal with them. If you apply some of the basic principles of collaboration, you can even begin to reduce the resistance.

Author and consultant Rick Maurer describes resistance to change as occurring on three levels. Understanding which level of resistance exists is the first step to knowing how to deal with it. Notice I did not say "overcome it." Thinking in terms of "overcoming resistance" usually stiffens the resistance. Consider the three levels of resistance that Maurer identifies.

LEVELS OF RESISTANCE

1 Lack of knowledge – "I don't understand it." *Provide information!*
2 Fear of consequences – "I don't like it!" *Embrace the concerns and address them.*
3 Deep-seated dislikes and disputes – "I don't like you!" *Find another approach or a different partner – this one is likely to fail!*

Once you have identified the level of resistance, look for the symptoms of resistance and then you can begin to make progress in dealing with the resistance to change that is thwarting your collaboration and partnership.

FORMS OF RESISTANCE TO CHANGE

- *Confusion*: a fog that makes it hard to hear that change is coming – *Explain clearly what the change is all about.*
- *Immediate criticism*: before people hear the details, they are against it – *Ask them to listen to the end before forming any opinions.*
- *Denial*: people refuse to see or accept that things are different – *Use examples to illustrate how things will be different.*
- *Malicious compliance*: they smile and seem to go along, only to reveal later that they don't – *Carefully watch their behavior and follow-up on promise actions to see that they are taken.*
- *Sabotage*: actions taken to inhibit or kill the change – *Enlist the help of the group or of specific change leaders to detect this behavior.*
- *Easy agreement*: people agree without much resistance, but may not realize what they are agreeing to – *Make sure they realize what it will mean to them.*
- *Deflection*: change the subject and maybe it'll go away – *Don't let this derail the change discussion.*
- *Silence*: hard to deal with because of no feedback – *Require each person involved in the change to describe how his or her situation will change.*

With credit to Rick Maurer, author of *Beyond the Wall of Resistance*, Bard, 1996

Interpersonal conflicts

A formidable obstacle to collaboration arises when a person is asked to work with people they don't particularly like. Resolving this one can be very difficult. One of the hardest things to do in business is to work with people you don't like or don't respect. The challenge of breaking down old bad feelings stops many collaborative efforts. There is no simple solution for this problem. One not-so-simple solution is to change the people involved.

Smart things
to say

If the people won't change, we'll
have to change the people.

Another of the difficulties that can undermine collaboration is conflict between individuals that goes unresolved too long. This can be caused by non-performers who want too much credit or strong performers who begin to feel (and behave) as if they are too important or deserve a disproportionate amount of the recognition for the collaboration's outcomes. Entrenched emotional positions are problems for partnerships. Such inter-personal difficulties require strong, positive leadership to address and resolve them. At times, some members of the group may actually have to be dismissed from the group if the problems cannot be resolved.

Smart quotes

"It is one of the most beautiful compensations of this life that no man can sincerely try to help another without helping himself."

Ralph Waldo Emerson

Know your collaborators

Getting to know your partners' skills, goals, interests, preferences, and work style is invaluable. Often, collaboration occurs among persons who already know each other well. When people don't know one another yet appreciate the value of collaborating, it helps to get them together to engage in non-threatening, simple tasks as icebreakers at the start of a partnership. Working on something simple provides a sense of achievement for the group and helps the partners get to know each other. The movie *Remember the Titans* provides a good, entertaining lesson in this principle, and was based on a true story.

SMART VOICES

"They must change who would be constant in happiness and wisdom."

Confucius

Techniques such as asking people to introduce themselves and give the group a couple of personal and professional tidbits is a good way to break the ice. If each person can relate a small success story from their life or career, and then share some personal insight, members of the group build a deeper understanding of each other. Knowing each other as people at first is more important than knowing them as partners or team members. That comes later.

Document agreements – publicly

During the course of building partnerships, agreements will be reached, both within the group and between groups. It is important to spell out commitments or agreements in writing, preferably on an easel in full sight of everyone. Doing so in this public way implies to the group an acceptance of what was written down unless some member of the group disputes it then and there. This step also minimizes misunderstandings and avoids later disagreements about what was done – either accidental or intentional. If agreement is being reached on most points and just a couple of issues are "hang-ups," then you can use a "parking lot" – a separate easel for recording the difficult-to-resolve issues. This permits progress on most points and identifies the sticky issues for further work at a future time.

Smart quotes

"Discovery consists of seeing what everybody has seen and thinking what no one else has thought."

Albert Szent-Gyorgi (Nobel Prize winner in biochemistry)

When people work together on something difficult, there will be times when the partners may be at odds with each other and don't bring up the real issues. These will fester and undermine the partnership's unity of purpose. Ultimately, such unresolved issues will limit or destroy collaboration. Because of this, it is important to regularly ask how the working relationship is doing. Tools to do this exists, but a simple one is a verbal (or even anonymous written) polling of people via a simple 5–6 question survey and plotting results on a chart (Fig. 7.3).

Answer with a rating from 1 to 5 on each question

1   Are all opinions being heard?

2   Are all participants being given an equal chance to participate?

3   How objectively are matters being considered?

4   How fairly are conclusions being reached?

5   How much of a sense of collaboration is there among this group?

6   Do you feel an important part of this group?

1=Not at all, 2= Somewhat, 3=About average, 4=Quite a bit, 5=Totally

For each answer, place a small x in the row for the rating number given in answer to a specific question. Clusters of xs will reveal how the group feels about its collaborative efforts. If the clusters are near the top of the chart, things are going well. If many are near the bottom, there are problems that must be resolved for a good collaborative result.

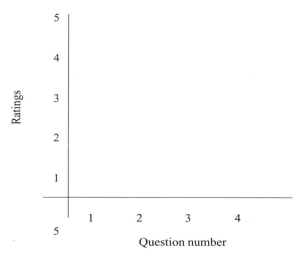

Fig. 7.3 Collaboration effectiveness

Choosing the right kind of partnership helps achieve success

Collaborate on what?

Collaboration is not a partnership cure-all. There is no need for a team, a partnership or a collaboration to turn on the lights, answer the telephone or turn down the thermostat. Sometimes a single person can and should do the job all alone. This is often faster and far more effective for simple jobs, and sometimes for jobs requiring a highly technical individual skill – such as surgery! The surgeon may need a team of assistants, but often only one person can make the incisions, and do the actual surgery most effectively.

Smart quotes

"Of all the virtues we can learn, no trait is more useful, more essential for survival, and more likely to improve the quality of life than the ability to transform adversity into an enjoyable challenge."

Mihaly Csikszentmihalyi

Collaboration occurs best only when people and partners believe they have common goals and can help one another achieve them. Here are a few examples.

- What do you want to achieve – specifically?

- Write it down and put numbers, dates, and names on this. If everyone is responsible, no one is responsible!

- Do you have similar ideas of how to get there and what you are willing to do to achieve those goals – and how to "get it done?"

- Balance is critical and difficult to achieve. Like a bank account, you have to make some deposits before you can make many withdrawals.

- Can all parties come to feeling a sense of ownership? This has to happen!

- Everybody must have a chance to "invest" and achieve buy-in with his or her thoughts, opinions, and feelings.

Smart quotes

"I have learned that success is to be measured not so much by the position that one has reached in life, as by the obstacles which one has overcome while trying to succeed."

Booker Washington

A single set of goals can be set by having them imposed by higher authority. While this may work for a single organization, it is not usually effective for two organizations from different companies. This is also not nearly as good as having the group(s) collaborate to agree upon them, but it is faster, and often happens anyway.

In many cases, the needs are clearly defined by external conditions – achieve something a customer wants; beat a competitor; solve a problem; etc. In these cases, setting the goals and objectives for partnership collaboration may not be too difficult, but getting all the people to buy into them may be very tough.

Define expected results, goals and objectives

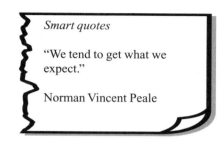

Smart quotes

"We tend to get what we expect."

Norman Vincent Peale

Unless partners work together to agree upon a set of goals, there is a danger that their efforts will be fragmented by pursuing slightly (or widely) different objectives. This is very disturbing since all may be working hard and effectively, but not with the same purpose. As time passes, they may realize these different purposes and goals are a problem, but by then they will have become committed to the particular one they were pursuing. This makes agreeing on a single set of common goals even more difficult. (It is not easy in the first place – and the more organizations and people involved, the harder it becomes!)

Set meaningful measures

Remember the section on measuring partnerships and Will Kaydos comments, "If you can't [*or won't*] measure it, you can't [*or won't*] manage it." [Additions are mine.] One way to clarify goals and objectives early is to determine the measures that are to be used. This will help force clarification of the specifics of the goal. Measures tend to create and reinforce behaviors. The old saying "What gets measured, gets done" has a lot of truth in it. Who is getting measured (and compensated) for what results, and who is doing the measuring?

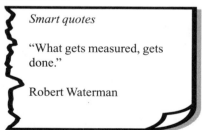

Smart quotes

"What gets measured, gets done."

Robert Waterman

Partners do best if they can devise their own measures and then keep track of progress themselves. When someone else – anyone else from the "outside" – creates the measures and keeps track, there can be a feeling of being watched, graded, policed and reported on. This is not the feeling you want to have among partners if they are to be effective collaborators.

Another common problem is that the measures don't measure what is really desired – or if they do – that what they measure is somehow altered by the measurement itself. This subject is close to the earlier topic of understanding the goals of the partnership. If the goals are clearly understood, the measures are easier (not necessarily easy!) to develop. The people who are partnering need to determine their own measures, and then verify that they are working toward the right goals and objectives. Few things are more demoralizing than to have a group of people who truly partner and collaborate to achieve their goal, only to discover it was the wrong goal!

Disagreement at the top

Another dangerous threat to partners collaborating is where the two (or more) organizations discover that there is disagreement or confusion about goals in other parts of their organization – especially if those other parts are top management! Work on this one early and check as you proceed in the partnership collaboration to make sure that the respective top management is still solidly on board with the goals, objectives, risks, rewards, and resource requirements. This is not something to discover in later stages, because things will certainly get ugly then!

> Smart things to say
>
> Always take a little more than your share of the blame and a little less than your share of the credit.

Collaboration takes time – and time is a perishable resource. The best ways of engaging a group of people to pursue a given set of objectives is for the group to reach consensus. Consensus takes time to develop. Some situa-

> "To maintain superior performance, you and your partner must be confident that your successful collaboration today will continue tomorrow."
>
> Jordan Lewis

SMART PEOPLE TO HAVE ON YOUR SIDE

tions are so urgent that time is scarce and the luxury of a full consensus-building process is not possible. In these cases, a leader must set the agenda and the goals for the group.

The partners then have to find how they can take ownership of those goals. If the organizations have been fairly open up until then, this may not be much of a problem, because most people will understand the sense of urgency and why it exists. If the organizations have not been working together very well to begin with, finding ways to collaborate is very hard until interpersonal relationships of some kind are established between the members of the respective partners. This takes time and energy for them to develop – by actually working together.

Collaboration is not the only way – but may be the best way

Nothing succeeds like success. Getting things done in any setting can create good feelings but not always the powerful kind created when a group achieves something together. How the results are achieved means as much to many people as how good the results are. That is why collaboration is such a satisfying way for partners to work together and get things done.

Smart quotes

"When we look for the good in others, we discover the best in ourselves."

Ralph Waldo Emerson

"If you have a penny and I have a penny, and we exchange pennies, you still have one cent and I still have one cent. But if you have an idea, and I have an idea and we exchange ideas, you now have two ideas and I have two ideas."

Anonymous

Another reason that collaborative success is valuable is that it provides the potential for synergy – that widely used but poorly understood word that results from the whole being much greater than the sum of the parts. Synergies are possible both within group collaboration and among several groups.

If a group of partners collaborate in the achievement of meaningful goals and they succeed, this creates a powerful force for the future. These people can then be spread among new groups to help them learn the kind of relationships and processes that lead to successful collaboration. The good feelings and sense of achievement can then be multiplied over and over. That is truly a great legacy to leave any organization!

8

New Directions, New Opportunities, Old Problems

WHAT DOES THE FUTURE HOLD, AND HOW WILL PARTNERSHIPS HELP YOU SUCCEED?

THE SIX SMARTEST THINGS TO KNOW ABOUT PARTNERSHIPS

No one is good enough to succeed alone.
Whoever chooses the best partners, wins!
Trust is a must – and a two-way street.
There has to be enough in it for both partners.
No support from the top means "no deal."
Power is poison to partnerships.

Now that you have read most of this book, you are much smarter about partnerships and alliances. There are several major points that must be mentioned again before leaving this large and important topic. This chapter is kind of a "smorgasbord" – a "catch-all" containing bits and pieces of information that need mentioning, explaining or repeating again and a few scattered pieces of new information.

Beauty may only be skin deep, but ugly goes to the bone

Not all partnerships work out. Some are just destined to fail. At times, there simply isn't enough in the partnership for both partners. When there is no commitment at the top of the partner organizations, difficulties don't get resolved. "Blame-placing" takes over. That is the beginning of the end.

Some people, in some companies just will not, or cannot be trustworthy partners. Somebody tries to double-cross the other partner. In other cases, one or the other partner doesn't either want to or know how to be a partner. As soon as you recognize one of these, watch out for yourself and your company.

Watch out for the *"you give and I take"* (phony) partners. Avoid them and if you can't avoid them, protect yourself at all times. Most important, don't waste your valuable time and that of your organization on these hopeless partnerships. These types of partnerships are ugly and just won't work.

Don't give up ... and don't become power-driven

Some partnerships work wonderfully. The partners are both much better off and are usually rewarded handsomely in the marketplace. These are the ones to understand and use as models. The bad ones will continue to make the word partnership a bad cliché at times – but don't let that stop you.

There is another characteristic of partnerships that often goes unnoticed. They are cyclical – just like businesses are. What do I mean by that? Well, when times are good, partnerships are easier. There is more growth and more gain for both partners to share. When times turn bad, the worm turns.

During periods of economic contraction or recession, the temptation to wield power (which I hope you recall is "poison to partnerships" by now) is almost irresistible. The larger the company and the tougher the times, the more likely the interpretation of partnerships will be, *"you give and I take."*

When DaimlerChrysler needed better earnings, it simply held its hand out to its (so-called) supplier partners asking for five percent upfront and ten percent over the next two years. This is the "big bad wolf" form of partnership – *"if you don't let me in, I'll huff and I'll puff and I'll blow your house down."* Smart suppliers hang on, and hold out, hoping they can reason with the "big, bad wolf" but sometimes that just doesn't work.

Then you know two things – it was never really a partnership in the first place, and if you want to keep the business short term, you find a way to give what is required. Then you figure out how to find a better partner next time. Once a partnership has been poisoned this way, it will never be the same again.

Large publicly owned companies are the worst about this. They do whatever it takes to make Wall Street's estimated earnings. But what about the next quarter or the one after that? Edicts come down from the highest levels of the corporate tower – go get the money from the suppliers. That is why partner-

SMART PEOPLE
TO HAVE ON
YOUR SIDE

"Adversarial relationships work only if you never have to see or work with the bastards again."

Peter Drucker

ships must be supported with strong commitment from the highest levels of the corporation – and even then, that may not be enough. CEOs are dropping like flies, and if the CEO perceives that his/her job is at stake, all rational behavior flies out the window – along with it go the partnership commitments.

Always ask what else, or how else … or take an IOU

Your only hope is to avoid or survive these cyclical firestorms or to find win-win propositions that achieve the same end results. You can give an additional five percent discount if you can get more volume, more lead-time, more standardization, some relief on specifications, etc. You pick the amounts and selections, but choose the "how else can we do it" approach in the hope of salvaging the partnership – and the business.

Sometimes you can give "free goods or services" along with incremental purchases, and in the process, it costs you the *cost value* (on the freebies) but the customer gets the benefit of the *price value*. Thus you use your profit margin on the free goods to be able to give more apparent value than actual value.

When companies encounter hard times, and the economy is not the culprit, they often resort to these same tactics. Kmart was notorious a few years back for "taking the money" however it could get it. Many suppliers decided that they didn't need that kind of partner, and left Kmart with a decidedly second-rate group of suppliers in some product categories.

Making your fiscal quarter or year earnings by taking those earnings out of your supplier partners' pockets to put it in yours is not a good idea – or a viable long-term strategy. Even industry leaders like Home Depot are suffering from supplier ill will because of poor partnership practices. Beware – *what goes around comes around* – and it will get you in the end.

"... auctions tend to undermine relationships with suppliers. Sellers feel exploited by the process, and when the event is over, they are less trusting of the buyer. As one supplier put it, '[The buyer] talks about a relationship being a partnership, and this [the auction] really takes that away' ..."

Sandy Jap, "Going, Going, Gone" *Harvard Business Review*, November–December, 2000

SMART VOICES

Globalization – cultural issues

Establishing partnerships in unfamiliar cultures is a challenge under the best of circumstances – and yet this is just where you need them! Practices that are accepted in one culture might be offensive or insulting in another. Behaviors that are commonplace in certain cultures are unacceptable in others. The concept of a "fair deal" can be a serious trap if practitioners from Western cultures assume their interpretation of "fair" will hold up in Asian or Latin American cultures.

Chinese "partners" have been notorious for not holding to their end of the bargain, and without a "rule of law" analogous to Western practices, there is nowhere to turn for "enforcement." Scary, right? Financial institutions in places like Thailand have deemed certain loan obligations as unpayable – but then effectively said, "so what," just let it ride.

"To fully exploit the opportunities open to it, a company today must have an ability to conceive, shape and sustain a wide variety of strategic partnerships."

Yves Doz and Gary Hamel

SMART VOICES

"Manana is good enough for me" was the line in an old song. That may also be the philosophy of your Latin American partner, even if that doesn't fit with your schedules or deadlines. Are you ready for a siesta after lunch – for the rest of the afternoon? They are! Are you prepared to deal with *lubricacione* or what is called a "bribe" in some countries? Such payments may be common in other cultures – just a part of doing business. Your local partner will know how that works, and if it needs to be done to make things work. Inflation in underdeveloped countries can be many times that of the more prosperous markets, making black markets, cash transactions and bribery common business practices. Are you ready for those kinds of partnerships?

Even though the Corrupt Business Practices Act, which prohibits bribery and extortion, was passed by the US in the late 1970s, it is just now being adopted by leading Asian countries. Expect slow adoption and weak enforcement. Old habits and practices die hard.

Humanization – people issues

Kathy Lee Gifford raised the awareness of Americans to the workplace cultures of foreign clothing producers, and the world will never be the same. But, in many cases, even the less desirable sewing shops were a better place for teenaged girls than the alternatives – street prostitution or starvation. The challenge is that humanitarian practices shouldn't be different in different places but they are. Who will realize these things in your partnership?

SMART VOICES

"For industry giants and ambitious start-ups alike, strategic partnerships have become central to competitive success in fast-changing global markets.

Yves Doz and Gary Hamel

"More and more manufacturers will band together with cadres of suppliers to create semi-private exchanges… They are creating a shared business infrastructure with their suppliers. Other manufacturers are going to have to play catch up."

Source: conversation "Competing for Supply," *Harvard Business Review*, February 2001

SMART VOICES

Finding and working with partners means learning about all of these issues in advance. Labor laws vary from country to country, from continent to continent. If your partner violates them, are you liable? Who knows? You'd better know, if you want these new kinds of partnerships to survive and prosper.

How about the moral issues right at home? Your partner's company is in trouble. It faces sexual harassment charges, and other discrimination lawsuits. How far must it – can it – go to survive and prosper? What about skyrocketing benefit costs? Cutting healthcare benefits for retirees has become a common practice. Is it inhumane? Perhaps it is, but if the partner company did not survive at all, those benefits would be gone, and all of the current employees' jobs along with them – and maybe your source of supply as well!

Partnerships are for good times and bad ones. Good partnerships are moral. Bad ones are immoral. When is it fair to ask a partner to make sacrifices you are not willing to make? Will the top management take an unpaid layoff of 4–5 weeks when business conditions turn down? I don't think so. Of course they may not get such big bonuses, but no paycheck is a lot different than no bonus. Finding the way to feel like a partner while not being treated like one is a difficult task – maybe an impossible one.

Smart quotes

"Make something of yourself. Try your best to get to the top, if that's where you want to go, but know that the more people you try to take along with you, the faster you'll get there and the longer you'll stay."

James A. Autry

Bandwidth vs. attention spans – technology issues

High tech, high touch, high speed, high risk, high profit – these are all partnership and business and strategic issues. So your partner is "wired" to you. Great! Or is it? No more hiding the late production and short inventory on a critical item. No more fuzzy answers about when that order will ship or when that service will be completed. Are you ready for that – partner?

The era of the Internet has moved the connectivity and openness of information sharing to a whole new level. In days gone by, people could "bend the truth" without getting caught. Not any more! Now the elements of trust and trustworthiness are being put to the ultimate test. The question now will not be "when is the shipment I need going to arrive?" The question will be, "what in the hell are you going to do to get me what I need in time, because the way your schedules are setup now, that is not going to happen?" Kind of a different tone – right?

SMART PEOPLE
TO HAVE ON
YOUR SIDE

"Though ample experience ... indicates that trust produces better results than strong-arming another organization, some people regard trust as a concept best left to sociologists."

Jordan Lewis

But, if the parts of the system that are supposed to be working ahead of this time are doing their job, perhaps that question will come much less frequently. Internet technologies and close-knit partnerships now make it possible for partners to truly collaborate on planning, forecasting and making adjustments all throughout the supply chain – not just in one factory or

NETWORKED INCUBATORS AND THE NEW ECONOMY

A new partnership-building business model

"When properly designed, networked incubators combine the best of two worlds – the scale and scope of large, established corporations and the entrepreneurial spirit of small venture-capital firms – all while providing unique networking benefits. Because of this combination, we believe that networked incubators represent a fundamentally new organization model that is especially well suited for creating value and wealth in the new economy.

"The distinguishing feature of a networked incubator is that it has mechanisms to foster partnership among start-up teams and other successful Internet-oriented firms, thus facilitating the flow of knowledge and talent across companies and forging of marketing and technology relationships between them. With the help of such an incubator, start-ups can network to obtain resources, and partner with others quickly, allowing them to establish themselves in the marketplace ahead of competitors.

Morten Hansen, Henry Chesbrough, Nitin Nohria and Donald Sull. "Networked Incubators – Hothouses of the New Economy," *Harvard Business Review*, September–October, 2000

delivery process. If the retail trade's efforts on CPFR – that stands for Collaborative Planning, Forecasting and Requirements – works broadly like it is beginning to in a few places, then a whole new era of partnerships and Value Network management is at hand.

CPFR – A PROMISING NEW PARTNERSHIP TOOL

One of the hottest new partnership tools is an approach called Collaborative Planning Forecasting and Replenishment, or CPFR for short. What is it? CPFR is a cross-industry initiative designed to improve supplier-customer relationships through co-managing the planning and sharing of responsibility for the forecasting and replenishment of goods – primarily for retailers.

This process, developed by a group called the Voluntary Inter-industry Commerce Standards (VICS) Association, defines the best practices and protocols to make CPFR work for the partners who use it. This initiative began a few years ago with consultancy, Benchmark Partners (now named Surgency), large suppliers like Warner-Lambert and large customers like Wal*Mart, seeking better ways to stay in stock, reduce inventory, and improve communications. Supply chain software companies like Manugistics and several ERP software firms were also involved early in the CPFR process.

A pilot project involved Warner-Lambert's Listerine® mouthwash sold via Wal*Mart stores. The process was first used in a paper-based form and then demonstrated on a computer. In-stock positions for Listerine® rose from 87 to 98 percent, lead times dropped from 21 to 11 days, and sales increased $8.5 million over the test period even though the test was limited to one Warner-Lambert plant and only three Wal*Mart distribution centers. This was clearly a powerful partnership tool.

The purpose of CPFR is to reduce or eliminate uncertainty through improved communications between supply chain trading partners. The key word in the name is "collaborative."

This is not as surprising as it might seem, because true collaboration is rare enough within companies, and rarer still between companies!

The keys to making CPFR work require changes in behavior of the people at the partners – a real challenge. The difficulty is getting all of those using the process to consistently act in the spirit of the collaborative process. Trust is the issue in most collaborative partnerships and this one is no exception. If both partners in the CPFR process realize that the end consumer is their customer, and behave accordingly, the process can work wonders. When they don't, it makes only minor improvements.

Although they don't overtly call it CPFR, the Manco-Wal*Mart relationship is one of the more productive ones using this methodology. Why? Because the people act, feel and work like partners. That is the only way any of these new initiatives will realize the greatest benefits for the partners involved. Wal*Mart's RetailLink system allows its suppliers to have unparalleled visibility of the performance and status of the goods in Wal*Mart's stores and distribution system. This kind of open information sharing is a hallmark of partnership.

Sophisticated retailers like Wal*Mart are insisting on ever shorter shipping windows – now down to two days in some cases. These retailers will also share information more, and better than ever before, on retail movement of goods. The wise partner learns how to use this information flow to fine-tune the flow of materials in its Value Network. Using "community-based" merchandise assortments, Wal*Mart is tailoring the goods on the shelf to optimize the fit with the needs of each store. This can mean both increased sales and increased headaches for suppliers.

These are demanding times. Partnerships require that all of the partners in the Value Network understand their role and responsibility and perform consistently to expectations. Which brings us to a topic that is appropriate

HOW TO MAKE CPFR HAPPEN

- Solicit a senior management champion;
- dedicate resources (i.e., project leaders, etc.);
- pick your pilot (and partner);
- establish the win-win potential; and
- dive into the process (to align relationships with partners, create value, and compete more effectively).

Source: "Supply Chain Collaboration – Close Encounters of the Best Kind" *BusinessWeek*, March 26, 2001

to touch again – expectations. More partnerships fail because of misunderstood or unrealized expectations than any other cause – except two – a *poor choice* of partners upfront, and a *lack of trust* once underway.

Defining expectations is not always easy. Nor is it painless. But it is better to do this as soon and as well as possible or you will suffer unpleasant consequences. I always remember a very short lecture given to me by a senior manager from Wal*Mart early in my career. His name was Bill Durflinger, and what he said to me was, "We have a simple policy at Wal*Mart. We buy. You ship. You don't ship, we don't buy."

Then he went on, "You are assuming a great responsibility by accepting our business. That responsibility is not just to Wal*Mart, but to Wal*Mart's customers – and it is to have what we planned to be on the store shelf for sale when they want to buy it. Don't take that responsibility lightly."

Obviously his words made a great impression on me since I can quote them 20 years later! I can only hope that a few of the words I have put in this book will be as memorable to you.

Conclusion

Now we have come to the end of the book. What are the smart things to know about partnerships that you should take away from this book? You should make a list of 5–10 of the points that are memorable and relevant to you. Then read on to see if others are recalled as I reprise some of the most important ones.

It is important to understand how to build partnerships.

They can be very powerful and no one can be good enough at everything in today's rapidly changing new economy of global competition.

Partnerships are so powerful because the good ones result from a shared vision.

They use the collective wisdom and passion of all the partners' people working toward a shared set of goals and objectives, realizing that there is something in it for them if they succeed.

How to get started forming partnerships

- Choosing the right potential partners is the first, and most critical step.

- Then matching cultures, goals, aspirations, resources, risks/rewards, etc. comes next.

- Finally, defining and agreeing on expectations is a must for success.

- Then sit down and start discussing all of the above. Review it up and down and across your organization and ask your prospective partner to do the same.

Then get started – think BIG, but try small, then adjust and keep going. If it is worth doing, it is worth doing NOW!

- Use a checklist for choosing partners; observe the dos and don'ts of mismatched cultures, power and risk/reward imbalances, etc.

- Develop your own assessment and checklist.

- Be sure to consider the Ws – Why, Which, Win-win, Will, Way, Walk, When, Who.

- And, when partnerships don't work right – use these steps again to see what can be done?

- Expect obstacles and look for opportunities for partnering.

- Find support from senior management to help move obstacles. Imagine the potential opportunities if you succeed.

- Stay positive until you either make it work or decide to take it apart.

Learn why, where, and when to use partnerships as part of strategic outsourcing and why strong, effective outsourcing depends on partnering:

- *Why* (strategy) – to beat the competition, make more money, do it faster, better, and always – to serve the customer better.

- *Where* (execution) – where you can't do it alone (which is almost always), so you can concentrate on what you are best at doing.

- *When* (need) you cannot afford to be good enough at everything, choosing what to be good at and who to trust for the things you're not good at is critical.

- *When* (timing) – as soon as you realize you should – like right now!

Understand the reasons for using partnerships and outsourcing – how and when to use alliances, partnerships, different forms of working together:

The old 4–5–6 memory trick

The 4 types of partnerships

- Partnerships with suppliers

- Partnerships with customers

- Partnerships with employees and associates

- Special partners, personal or professional

The 5 kinds of business relationships

- Partnerships

- Alliances

- Joint ventures

- Transactions

- Mergers and acquisitions

The 6 categories (and reasons) for partnering

- Marketing and/or customer access

- Technology and/or proprietary know-how

- Capacity and/or resources

- Skills and/or talent

- Financial and/or economics

- Special situations

Always remember these ten smart partnership priorities

- *Choice.* Choose carefully and wisely – is this an important and valuable partner?

- *Willingness.* Are you willing to be a partner, and is your partner?

- *Trust.* Does trust already exist or can it be built (or rebuilt)?

- *CHIPs*. Character, Honesty, Integrity and Principles – must be there – are they?

- *Fit*. Strategically, structurally and culturally – can you both make it work?

- *Communication*. And information sharing – will you – and will they?

- *Goals*. Are they shared, understood and in a consistent direction?

- *3Rs*. Risks, Rewards, and Resources – are they fairly balanced and adequately understood?

- *Commitment*. Does it exist at the top, middle and bottom and across functions in both organizations? Are there "champions" or at least sponsors in both organizations?

- *Measures*. Do you both know and agree "what is success" and how you'll know it when you achieve it – and are you both willing to stick to it through good times and bad? Can you imagine the form of partnership this should take?

And last, but certainly not least, never forget these:

THE SIX SMARTEST THINGS TO KNOW ABOUT PARTNERSHIPS

1 No one is good enough to succeed alone.
2 Whoever chooses the best partners, wins!
3 Trust is a must – and a two-way street.
4 There has to be enough in it for both partners.
5 No support from the top means "no deal."
6 Power is poison to partnerships.

Bibliography and Reading List

"Agile Competitive Behavior – Examples from Industry," *Agile Manufacturing Enterprise Forum Working Papers*, July 1994.

"Competing for Supply," conversation, *Harvard Business Review*, February, 2001.

"Hardball Is Still GM's Game," *BusinessWeek*, August 8, 1994, p. 26.

"How a U.S. Manufacturer is Beating Very Tough Foreign Competition," John L. Mariotti in *Boardroom Reports,* March 1, 1988.

"Low Wages No Longer Give Competitive Edge," *Wall Street Journal*, March 16, 1988.

"McDonald's Conquers the World," *Fortune*, October 17, 1994, pp. 103–116.

"Partnerships: Creating Synergy," training materials for the course Strategies for High-Involvement Leadership. Developmental Dimensions International, Pittsburgh, 1994.

"Some Cool Thoughts for Hot Summer Days," *Inside Retailing* June 20, 1994.

"Supply Chain Collaboration – Close Encounters of the Best Kind," *BusinessWeek*, March 26, 2001.

"View from the Top: John Mariotti Speaks Out," *TEI Newsletter,* July–August 1990.

"A Practical Guide to Alliances: Leapfrogging the Learning Curve – A Perspective for U.S. Companies." *Viewpoint*, Booz·Allen and Hamilton, 1993.

Arlen, Jeffrey, "Cyber Trust: Will It Work?" *Discount Store News,* July 1994.

Champy, James, "What Comes After Business Reengineering?" *Index SMI Review,* Fourth Quarter 1993, pp. 8–9.

Covey, Stephen R. (1994) *First Things First*, Simon and Schuster, New York.

Covey, Stephen R. (1990) *Principle Centered Leadership*, Simon and Schuster, New York.

Covey, Stephen R. (1989) *The Seven Habits of Highly Effective People*, Simon and Schuster, New York.

Daly, James, Editor-in-Chief, *Business 2.0*, December 26, 2000.

Das, T. K. and Teng, Bing-Sheng, Baruch College, CUNY, "Between Trust and Control: Developing Confidence in Partner Cooperation in Alliances," *Academy of Management Review*, 1998.

Dent, Stephen M. (1999) *Partnering Intelligence*, Davies-Black.

Doz, Yves and Hamel, Gary (1998) *Alliance Advantage*, Harvard Business School Press, Boston MA.

Drucker, Peter F. "The Five Deadly Business Sins," *Wall Street Journal*, October 21, 1993.

Drucker, Peter F. "The Network Society," *Wall Street Journal*, March 29, 1995

Drucker, Peter F. (1999) *Management Challenges for the 21st Century*, Harper, New York.

Drucker, Peter F., quoted by Mike Verespej, "Only the CEO can Make Employees Kings" *IndustryWeek*, November 16, 1998.

Drucker, Peter F. *(1954) The Practice of Management*, Harper and Row, New York.

Enslow, Beth, VP, Descartes Systems Group, from "The Glass Pipeline," *Supply Chain Management Software Supplement,* Cahners, 2000.

Fisher, Roger, and Ury, William (1981) *Getting to Yes*, Houghton Mifflin, New York.

Friedman, Thomas, remarks made at Cleveland (OH, USA) Council on World Affairs, October 4, 2000.

Friedman, Thomas (2000) *The Lexus and the Olive Tree*, Anchor Books, New York.

Godfrey, A. Blanton (1993) "Ten Clear Trends for the Next Ten Years," in *Profiting from Total Quality*, The Conference Board, New York.

Graham, Mark, *IndustryWeek,* March 5, 2001.

Hamel, Gary, and Prahalad, C. K. "Strategic Intent," *Harvard Business Review,* May–June 1989.

Hamel, Gary, and Prahalad, C. K. "Strategy as Stretch and Leverage," *Harvard Business Review,* March–April 1993, pp. 75–84.

Hamel, Gary, and Prahalad, C. K. (1994) *Competing for the Future*, Harvard Business School Press, Boston, MA.

Hamel, Gary, in "Reinventing Competition," *Executive Excellence,* January, 2000.

Hamel, Gary (2000) *Leading the Revolution*, Harvard Business School Press, Boston, MA.

Hammer, Michael, and Champy, James (1993) *Reengineering the Corporation*, HarperCollins Books, New York.

Hammer, Michael "Reengineering Work: Don't Automate, Obliterate," *Harvard Business Review,* July–August 1990, pp. 104–112.

Hansen, Morten; Chesbrough, Henry; Nohria, Nitin and Sull, Donald, "Networked Incubators – Hothouses of the New Economy" *Harvard Business Review,* September–October, 2000.

Howard, Ann, and Wellins, Richard (1994) *High-Involvement Leadership – Changing Roles or Changing Times*, Development Dimensions International and Leadership Research Institute, Pittsburgh.

Jap, Sandy, "Going, Going, Gone" *Harvard Business Review,* November–December, 2000.

Kahl, Jack, "The Ethics of Partnership," *Duck Tales,* November–December 1993.

Kaydos, Will (1991) *Measuring, Managing, and Maximizing Performance*, Productivity Press, New York.

Kaydos, Will (1999) *Operational Performance Measurement*, St Lucie Press.

Kelly, Jim, chairman and CEO, UPS, in "Managing the Speed of Business," *Executive Excellence*, January, 2000.

Levitt, Theodore (1986) *The Marketing Imagination*, The Free Press, New York.

Lewis, Jordan(1990) *Partnerships for Profit: Structuring and Managing Strategic Alliances*, The Free Press, New York.

Lewis, Jordan (1995) *The Connected Corporation*, The Free Press, New York.

Lewis, Jordan (1999) *Trusted Partners*, The Free Press, New York.

Lynch, Clifford F., "Managing the Outsourcing Relationship," *Supply Chain Management Review*, September–October, 2000.

Maltz, Arnold, assistant professor, New Mexico State University in "Switch Partners or Keep Dancing?" *Transportation and Distribution,* July 1997.

Mariotti, John L., (1997) *The Shape Shifters – Continuous Change for Competitive Advantage*, Wiley, New York.

Mariotti, John L., (1996) *The Power of Partnerships*, Blackwell, Cambridge.

Maurer, Rick (1996) *Beyond the Wall of Resistance*, Bard, Dallas, TX.

Maurer, Rick (1992) *Caught in the Middle*, Productivity Press, Cambridge, MA.

McGregor, Douglas (1985) *The Human Side of Enterprise*, McGraw-Hill, NY.

McLean, Bethany, "Merging at INTERNET SPEED," *Fortune*, November 8, 1999.

Melohn, Tom (1994) *The New Partnership*, Omneo, an imprint of Oliver Wight Publications, Essex Junction, NH.

Mentzer, John T., Foggin, James H. and Golicic, Susan L., "Collaboration – The Enablers, Impediments, and Benefits" *Supply Chain Management Review,* September–October, 2000.

Morris, Tom (1997) *If Aristotle Ran General Motors*, Henry Holt and Company, New York.

Nasser, Jac, CEO, Ford Motor Co. in *Fortune,* December 18, 2000.

Peters, Thomas J. (1992) *Liberation Management*, Alfred A. Knopf, New York.

Peters, Thomas J., and Waterman, Robert H. (1982) *In Search of Excellence*, Harper and Row, New York.

Peters, Tom (1987) *Thriving on Chaos*, Alfred A. Knopf, New York.

Prahalad, C. K., and Hamel, Gary. "The Core Competence of the Corporation," *Harvard Business Review,* May–June 1990 pp. 79–91.

Reina, Dennis and Michelle, (1999) *Trust and Betrayal in the Workplace*, Berrett-Koehler, SF.

Rogers, Robert, COO, Development Dimensions International in *The Psychological Contract of Trust.*

Senge, Peter (1990) *The Fifth Discipline*, Doubleday Books, New York.

Shelton, Ken "Partners: Worth Their Weight in Gold." *Executive Excellence* 10, no. 11, November 1993, p. 2.

Shewmaker, Jack "Partnership in the 90s." Presentation to the International Mass Retailers Association convention, 1990.

Smith, Fred, chairman, president and CEO FedEx, in "New Connections," *Executive Excellence* January, 2000.

Sonnenberg, Frank K. "Managing with a Conscience." *Industry Week,* August 16, 1993.

"New and Noteworthy," *Soundview Book Summaries,* January 2001.

Stalk, George, Evans, Philip, and Shulman, Lawrence E. "Competing on Capabilities: The New Rules of Corporate Strategy." *Harvard Business Review,* March–April 1992, pp. 57–69.

Stalk, George, Jr "Time – the Next Source of Competitive Advantage." *Harvard Business Review,* July–August 1988, pp. 41–51.

Sujansky, Joanne G. (1991) *Power of Partnering: Vision, Commitment, and Action*, Pfeiffer and Co. San Diego, CA.

Summitt, Pat (1998) *Reach for the Summit*, Broadway, New York.

Treacy, Michael, and Wiersma, Fred "Customer Intimacy and Other Value Disciplines" *Harvard Business Review,* January–February 1993, pp. 84–93.

Twenty-first Century Manufacturing Enterprise Strategy. An Industry Led View, vol. 1. Bethlehem, PA: *Iacocca Institute,* Lehigh University, 1991.

Walton, Sam with Huey, John (1992) *Made in America, My Story,* Doubleday Books, New York.

White, Andrew, vice-president of product strategy, Logility, quoted in *Business Week,* March 26, 2001.

Womack, James P., Jones, Daniel T., and Roos, Daniel (1990) *The Machine That Changed the World,* Rawson division of Macmillan, New York.

Womack, James, and Jones, Daniel. "From Lean Production to the Lean Enterprise." *Harvard Business Review,* March–April 1993, pp. 93–103.

Index